# Life in the New World

## PITTSTON, PENNSYLVANIA

BY MARY THERESA POLICARE

DORRANCE
PUBLISHING CO
EST. 1920
PITTSBURGH, PENNSYLVANIA 15238

Dorrance Publishing Co
585 Alpha Drive
Pittsburgh, PA 15238
Visit our website at *www.dorrancebookstore.com*

ISBN: 978-1-6386-7147-3
eISBN: 978-1-6366-1554-7

# *Foreword*

This historical record of Italian immigration details the story of a young man and his family coming to the United States of America in 1903 at age twenty-six, from their native village of Calimera, Calabrian Region, Italy, arriving at Ellis Island. Subsequently they travelled via the Lehigh Valley Railroad to Pittston, Pennsylvania, joining other members of their families who were earlier immigrants to the anthracite region. It is a chronicle of the next fifteen years of their lives, adaptation to the society in the New World, to establishing a family, to work, to education, and the importance of religious affiliation and practice.

The author, a third-generation Italian-American, relates a family's story of the challenges and disappointments, successes and failures, opportunities and frustrations of immigrants of all nationalities becoming contributing citizens in their new homeland in northeastern Pennsylvania. It presents the reality of the multi-cultural "melting pot" phenomenon, which provided the skeletal framework for the social and economic progress of all immigrants who flocked to the hardcoal fields of Pennsylvania, supplying the workforce that drove the Industrial Revolution and made the United States the pre-eminent economy in the world. It details the many businesses, professions, and industries of Pittston, via a walking tour of the city's main business district, during the first two decades of the twentieth century.

The real-life story involves tales of life and love, acceptance and progress, the strength and importance of the generic family in the small, thriving city of Pittston, which provided the atmosphere for personal advancement and accomplishment. It includes reflections on a family's despair upon the death of their father/husband, leaving a young wife and eleven children. The book includes the effects of the 1918 Influenza Epidemic, as well as the United States' entry into World War I, experienced by Pittstonians, as representative examples of American society.

"Life in the New World: Pittston, Pennsylvania" is extensively researched, and documented. It concludes its story of immigration and triumph in 1919, on the dawn of Prohibition in 1920.

Richard Fitzsimmons, Ph.D.

This book is dedicated to Rocco and Maria (Romano) Policare for their determination and fortitude to travel to the United States of America to make a better "Life in the New World" for their family and future generations.

In addition it is dedicated to all the immigrants from every country who worked in the coal mines and other industries to lay the foundation for this free, prosperous, and great country.

# Table of Contents

<h1 style="text-align:center">Acknowledgements</h1>

My brothers, Rocco, Joseph, and Thomas for their support and encouragement during the past three years, with providing information of our family's journey to America.

Stanley Holko, for his love, support, and encouragement to write this family story.

Eric Sklanka, for his expertise in editing this story. His patience and insight were helpful throughout the past year.

My cousin, Patricia Schillaci, for giving input after every chapter. Her insight and enthusiasm made me want to continue. Her knowledge of family history and accuracy of every birthdate was a great help.

Richard Fitzsimmons, Ph.D., his unwavering interest for the story to be written and undivided attention and guidance to help me with research. From getting information at the Pennsylvania State University Library and Ellis Island, he enabled me to write this story.

Danny Argo – Montedoro Society, Monsignor John Bendik – Catholic Church History, Ann Conroy and Maria Capolarella Montante – Oregon Section, Julio Caprari – Pittston Stove Works, Welsh Church and the Italian Christian Church, Bill and Essy Davidowitz – Jewish History, Denise Dommermuth – Pittston History, John Dziak – Sanborn Maps and Early Pittston History, Ron Faraday - Early Pittston Stores, Ann Hrobak – Editing, Ruth Jamieson – First

Presbyterian Church History, Mike Lizonitz – Research, Jim McFarland – Friendly Sons of Saint Patrick, Marty Moscatelli – Computer Technology, Ed Philbin – Railroad Information, Charles Siegel – Computer Technology, Bernie Stiroh – Research, Tom Supey – Coal Mining History, Robert Wolensky – Coal Mining History.

*Chapter 1*

## CALABRIA, SOUTHERN ITALY

My family, Rocco and Maria (Romano) Policare, came from the Calabria Region of Southern Italy. Calabria is separated from Sicily by the Strait of Messina. They lived in the town of Calimera, which means "good morning" in Greek. It is a very small town in the Grecian Salentino area of the Salenta peninsula in Italy. In addition to Italians, the inhabitants of Calimera speak in Greek dialect. The language, folklore, traditions, and history of Calimera, like those of the eight other cities in the area called Salentinian Greece, reveal significant Greek influence over the course of time, presumably from the time of Byzantine control or even the ancient Magna Graecia Colonization in the 8th century. In the park located in the center of town, there is a small monument containing an ancient attic burial stone, given by the city of Athens to Calimera in 1957. At the top of this monument is a motto referring to the burial stone, "Zeni sue n ise etto sti Calimera" meaning, "You are not a stranger here in Calimera," which underscores the close relationship and common origins of Calimera with the rest of the Greek civilization.

In Calimera the main source of work was farming. The residents grew crops of fruits and vegetables to sell in the local markets. With the very warm temperatures in this region, olives and grapes provided a good source of income. The grapes picked were transported to larger cities to produce wine, which then would be shipped to different areas in Italy, as well as other countries. They had an olive press in the town square to extract the oil for shipment. This further produced the best grade of olive oil.

The town of Calimera is very small, with a few cobblestone and cement buildings on each side of the dirt road. The stores contained the basic goods: tools for farming, materials for sewing, food products, and leather goods. Women from each family would serve as midwives when needed at childbirth. The one doctor had a supply of useful remedies and the basic drugs that were available. When people became ill and the doctor was a distance, they would rely on home remedies for recovery. Calimera had a very self-sufficient lifestyle.

At the end of the street, there was a stable for horses and donkeys, the only modes of transportation. When the men wanted to go to the sea to fish, it took many hours of travel. In the meantime, the women of Calimera washed clothes in the stream and filled buckets to have drinking and bathing water in their homes. Everything was in walking distance, and life was simple. The hills in the region were always beautiful, with a variety of crops and trees growing there.

There was one Catholic parish, St. Mary's Catholic Church located on a small hill outside of town. The entrance of the church had three steps in front and a long porch the width of the building. Two double doors clad with wooden handles completed the entrance. On the top of the pitched roof was a cross. The nave of the church was approximately sixty feet in length and fifty feet wide, with a small wooden altar for the celebration of the Eucharist. Above the altar was a cement roof painted pale blue, the remainder of the roof was wood. The altar stood on a base shaped like a small bush, adorned with carved leaves. It was always adorned with beautiful white linens edged in lace made by the women of the church. The tabernacle (which means dwelling place) was a small embellished wood cabinet in the center of the altar. Above the altar on the wall was a beautiful wooden highly polished Crucifix. Wooden candle sticks on each side of the tabernacle matched the embellishment on the tabernacle. On the right wall, to the side of the altar, was a picture of the Holy Family painted by a woman from Calimera. It was encased in a wooden frame with engraved leaves to match the base of the altar. There were movable wooden benches on each side of the wooden floor. Sunlight would shine through four windows placed high on each side of the church.

Sunday was a holy day, and everyone refrained from work and attended services. Families knew each other, and after Mass they would gather together in the courtyard.

The homes were very small and were constructed of mud and cobble stone. Usually they consisted of four rooms: a living room, kitchen, and bedrooms. Because of the warm temperature of southern Italy, heating the homes was not a major concern. Their clothes and shoes were handmade, and sewing was taught from generation to generation. Their source of water was the local stream, and they raised chickens and other livestock for food. They had large families and were ready and willing to help each other. If any family was in need, the parish would announce the name and the parishioners would help them.

The small one-room schoolhouse, located next to the church, provided the basic skills of reading, writing, and arithmetic up to the sixth grade. If any family wanted their children to further their education, the family would have to go to a larger city. Many could not afford to send their children to a larger city, therefore their children were only provided with basic education. Greek and Italian were the languages spoken in Calimera.

Everything was in walking distance, and life was simple. Girls learned everything from their mothers and were married young. Boys worked alongside their fathers to learn the family trade. It was the custom to have arranged marriages. Many did not want arranged marriages and would rather marry someone they knew from their hometown.

In the late 1800s and the early 1900s, many Italians left Italy for Argentina and the United States of America. Poverty and overpopulation were both big reasons Italians sought new places to live.

Many Italians worked in rural areas and on farms, but the soil was becoming depleted and it was hard to grow any crops. Because of this, there were very few jobs in Italy (and especially southern Italy). Since there was such little food and so few jobs, diseases like cholera and malaria were making people ill. Since the conditions in Italy were so poor, coming to America gave Italians an opportunity to find work and make money to save and send home to their families. Another reason Italians immigrated to America was that natural disasters were unusually frequent in Italy at this time. These disasters wiped away entire cities and killed hundreds of thousands of people. Two volcanos that erupted in the early 1900s were Mount Etna and Mount Vesuvius.

By 1900 Italy was a relatively new country with little sense of national direction. Italy had for centuries been divided up into separate states, such as the Papal State, Venice, and Kingdom of the Two Sicilies. But from 1861 on, these states all came together with one king as their leader. In 1871 Rome was made the capital of Italy. So by 1900, Italy was barely thirty-years-old as a nation.

With no obvious chance of progress, many Italians simply left the country. America was the most popular choice of those who wished to emigrate. Between 1876 and 1926, nine million Italians emigrated there. A further 7.5 million emigrated to other parts of Europe.

Another reason why Italians left Italy was grape phylloxera. It is a pest of commercial grapevines worldwide, originally native to eastern North America. In the late 19th century, the phylloxera epidemic destroyed most of the vineyards for wine grapes in Europe, most notably in France.

Some of the early Italian families to leave southern Italy were the Romano and Policare families. Although it was going to be a new unknown experience, they made the decision for a better life for their families with more opportunities for future generations.

Carlo and Victoria Romano had a large family that lived at the edge of Calimera near the stream. They had a few cows and were very generous to others needing milk. Their oldest daughter Anna married Frank Policare. The Romano and Policare families were very close and continued their friendship because of the marriage of some of their sons and daughters. Anna, their eldest daughter, knew Frank all of her life.

Anna had short brown hair and oval brown eyes with little green speckles near the center. She had an olive complexion and a sweet smile. She worked in the fields alongside everyone else. When she wasn't working in the fields, she was helping her mother with the other children and cooking for the family.

Frank Policare was very good-looking with broad shoulders and a muscular body. He had wavy dark hair, hazel eyes with long eyelashes, a square jawline, and beautiful white teeth. He had a dimple in his chin and a wide grin and smile. His hands were strong because of hard work on the farm and picking the grapes. He was adventurous, bold, and daring. He loved his family and would protect them always.

Frank, like others in southern Italy, had a vision. He needed to leave his homeland to make a better life in America. There wasn't any other choice for him. Some relatives chose to relocate in Argentina. Frank was one of the first in his immediate family to make the two-week trip by boat from Naples, Italy to the United States of America. His goal, like many before him, was to start a new life and earn enough money to send to his family in Italy, so others could make the journey. He married Anna before he left for America. She stayed in Italy while Frank traveled to America to find work in the anthracite coal mines of northeastern Pennsylvania.

In 1898 Frank arrived in New York and took the train from New Jersey to Pittston, Pennsylvania. A few friends and relatives from Italy met him at the train station in Pittston. He needed a place to stay and found lodging at a hotel for immigrants and travelers. It was located at 71 North Main Street, Pittston, Pennsylvania. He came from a small town in Italy and now was among many different nationalities with the same goal to make a better life for themselves and their families.

Pittston, located in Luzerne County, is situated between Scranton and Wilkes-Barre. The city gained prominence in the late 19th and 20th centuries as an active anthracite coal mining city, drawing a large portion of its labor force from European immigrants.

It was settled in 1770 and incorporated as a borough April 30th, 1853. December 10th, 1894 it was incorporated as a city. Its total area is 1.7 square miles. At its peak in 1920, the population of Pittston was 18,497. The City of Pittston is named after William Pitt the Elder, First Earl of Chatham (born November 15th, 1708, died May 11th, 1778), a British Whig statesman who led Great Britain during the French and Indian War.

Pitt developed extraordinary parliamentary skills by which he dominated the British House of Commons. He displayed a commanding manner, brilliant rhetoric, and sharp debating skills that clearly utilized broad literary and historical knowledge. In recognition of his support of the American colonies, a number of cities and townships in the United States, including the cities of Pittsburgh, Pittston, and Pittston Township are named after him.

When Frank arrived, the people of Pittston were still in shock and mourning the death of fifty-eight men and boys. They died in the Twin Shaft Disaster that occurred on Sunday, June 28th, 1896. Residents in the Junction section of Pittston were rocked with what they believed to be explosions. The earth shook, doors and windows rattled, waking the people of Pittston and West Pittston, and some residents closer to the disaster were thrown from their beds. Witnesses at the time of the disaster said many were convinced it was an earthquake, but it soon became apparent that it was not a natural disaster. The town sirens and colliery whistles began to sound. Families quickly gathered at the Newton Coal Company's Twin Shaft Colliery.

Ninety miners were working in the Red Ash Vein, where it was estimated 200 acres of mine tunnels collapsed, killing fifty-eight workers 434 feet below the surface. The disaster left thirty-one widows and 101 children orphaned. Rescue efforts continued for days after the disaster only to fail, leaving all fifty-eight bodies, made up of chiefly Irish and Lithuanian immigrants, entombed forever. St. Mary, Help of Christian Church had thirty-two parishioners of the fifty-eight that perished in the massive cave-in.

Frank applied for a job at the Pennsylvania Coal Company. Because of his strong muscular appearance, he was granted a position as an unskilled laborer. In the beginning, he was on the early shift but many times had to work through the night. He would take extra hours to save money to send to his family for passage to America.

One of the many needs of the coal miner was good hard timber to be used as props. In the early 20th century, good timber was hard to come by, as most of the collieries had used up the local supplies. The mining company bought timber from suppliers.

After the timber was purchased, it had to be hauled to the colliery, where it would be placed in the prop yard or in the storage yard for uncut timber. When the miners needed a prop or collar for roof support, they had to measure and cut the long length of timber to the size required. All handling of the timbers was done by hand, using a tool called timber dog, a metal handhold hammered into the timber. One miner places the prop under the roof while the laborer digs out the dirt with his pick. The other man waits to hammer in a wedge to make a tight fit between the roof and floor.

Soon other family members would be arriving from Italy. Frank worked to pay for their passage.

*Chapter 2*

## ANTHRACITE COAL MINES

Pennsylvania was important because of the large amounts of anthracite coal found in the north, central, and southern coal fields. These included Lackawanna, Luzerne, Columbia, Carbon, Schuylkill, Northumberland counties, and the northeast corner of Dauphin County.

With the boom of the anthracite industry in the late nineteenth century, more miners and laborers were needed to meet the demand. The ever-resourceful coal operators, who had to deal with a shortage of American labor that was spreading throughout the country, turned to European immigrants who flooded the country by the millions looking for the American dream. The operators saw the influx as a new source of employees who were willing to work hard for less money than any American would. Thus the mining of coal became a job that was predominantly done by people who came to America to find work and refuge. At the time, the majority of mine workers and laborers in the area were Welsh and Irish. It wasn't until the 1870s and 1880s that residents of countries like Poland and Italy began to immigrate to America and make their way to the Pennsylvania coal mines.

After the Twin Shaft Disaster of 1896 in Pittston, Pennsylvania, miners in the region pointed to the ongoing safety hazards that they faced and the negligence of mine operators as a fundamental justification for unionization.

Other issues that executives were unwilling to negotiate included day-to-day leases of company homes, the practice of "docking," a percentage of the value of coal for its impurities, automatic fee deductions from workers' pay for the company doctor, and wages that had dropped or remained stagnant for years.

From the mid-nineteenth to the early twentieth century, nothing fueled the United States of America like anthracite coal. Coal power was an efficient and cost-effective way to heat homes. It also powered steam locomotives and the factories that produced items that built America. Throughout the Industrial Revolution, coal was quite literally the bedrock of the nation's progress. It is estimated that in the United States, there is enough coal to last for 2,500 years. Out of fifty states, twenty-five of them contain coal, but the largest of these fields is in the Appalachian coal area, which ranges from Alabama north to Pennsylvania and Ohio. By 1890, the United States of America and Pennsylvania became one of the largest coal producers in the world.

In 1897 a contingent of sheriffs' deputies fired upon an unarmed procession of striking mine workers who were marching between the patch town of Harwood and Lattimer in Luzerne County. The deputies killed nineteen and wounded many workers, immigrants from Eastern Europe who protested an "alien tax" imposed by the Assembly. They were proponents of better conditions in their mines. Both the Twin Shaft Disaster and the Lattimer Massacre resulted in great unity among mine workers who began to listen to labor leader John Mitchell's message: Unite.

John Mitchell, born in 1870 in Braidwood, Illinois, was a second-generation Irish immigrant. Orphaned when he was only six-years-old, John began working in the coal mine to support his family. John worked in and with the coal industry his whole life. When he was fifteen-years-old, he joined the Knights of Labor in 1885 and was a founding member of the United Mine Workers of America in 1890. He was elected District 12 secretary-treasurer in 1895. He was made an international union organizer in 1897 and was elected an international vice president the same year.

In September 1898, Mitchell became acting president of UMWA after president Michael Ratchford resigned to become a member of the United States Industrial Commission. Mitchell won election outright in 1899. One of Mitchell's earliest challenges in the United Mine Workers of America was to help incorporate new workers from various ethnicities into the union. There were numerous language barriers, as well as cultural biases and outright prejudices, to be overcome. He was a United States labor leader and president of the UMWA from 1898 to 1908.

Labor activity was notoriously dangerous at this time, but this was also a period of growth for the union. The number of members grew almost tenfold, from 34,000 to 300,000 during John Mitchell's term.

The Coal strike began on May 12th, 1902, also known as the "Anthracite Coal Strike," was a strike by the United Mine Workers of America in the anthracite coalfields of eastern Pennsylvania. Miners asked for higher wages, shorter workdays, and the recognition of their union. The strike threatened to shut down the winter fuel supply to all major cities and close down every hard coal operation in state of Pennsylvania. On June 2nd, 1902, the maintenance workers consisting of firemen, pump men, and engineers joined the strike.

Since the owners of the mines were equally committed to a perpetuation of a status quo, a stalemate ensued. Four months later, the summer heat was fast dissipating, but still antagonists were as far apart as ever. Since there was no substitution that could be used as fuel, the entire nation became alarmed. With the stockpiles nearly exhausted, basic industries were in danger of collapse. Home owners everywhere began to fear the coming winter. In the crisis, the public officials speculated on who were at fault but did little to relieve the situation.

Behind the scenes, there was one person working quietly toward a solution. He was The Reverend John J. Curran, the pastor of Holy Savior Roman Catholic Parish, Wilkes-Barre. A friend of John Mitchell, the leader of the United Mine Workers of America, the priest remembered well the eight years he had spent as a breaker boy and as a mule driver. From the day that he had left the mines at the age of sixteen, he had been convinced of the justice of the laborers' cause. After his ordination in August 22nd, 1887, Father Curran openly promoted the formation of union locals. When strikes were called, and there were many, he was always to be found on the side of the miner. He knew that bad as conditions were, they were bound to get worse unless and until his friends defeated the stubborn owner-operators. John Mitchell shared his views, and in 1902, it became their do-or-die effort.

While the union head strengthened the resolve of the ranks, Father Curran took upon himself the equally difficult task of improving the public image of the strikers. From the pulpit, he attacked the manifest evils of the age; to the press, he gave numerous interviews defending the rights of organized labor in general and the hard coal miners in particular; with his pen, he wrote an avalanche of letters to the leaders of government and industry seeking their support for the down trodden. Though the vast majority of the influential people of America wrote off his intervention as the work of a radical, President Theodore Roosevelt was not one of them.

Impressed by the case Reverend Curran made for the anthracite miners, the Chief Executive summoned the owners to the White House on October 3rd, 1902 and asked them to give serious consideration to the demands of the employees. The group adamantly refused to do so. Justifiably angered by their obstinacy, President Roosevelt turned to Father Curran. Between them they devised a plan to break the impasse. On October 16th, 1902, binding arbitration was proposed and a blue-ribbon presidential commission was named. With public sentiment in favor of a solution and with John Mitchell's acceptance of the panel, the mine owners capitulated, thereupon the strike ended.

The anthracite coal strike of 1902 resulted in a victory for the hard coal miners with a ten percent increase in wages and one-hour reduction in the workday. The miners believed that they deserved the right to have a say in their working conditions, health and safety issues, working hours, and rate of pay.

For five months, the investigation into Pennsylvania's coal industry continued. The Anthracite Coal Strike Commission, set up by President Theodore Roosevelt, held hearings at the Lackawanna County Courthouse in Scranton; testimony was taken and conclusions were formed. When all of the evidence was in, the Commission announced its findings, and on March 23rd, 1903, the United Mine Workers, John Mitchell and Father Curran, won a deserved victory, the first time that the concept of social justice intruded into the Lackawanna and Wyoming valleys.

The mine owners refused to recognize the United Mine Workers of America but were required to agree to a six-man arbitration board, consisting of equal members of labor and management representation with the power to settle labor disputes. The Anthracite Coal Strike Commission estimated that during the anthracite strike, the coal and railroad companies lost about seventy-four million dollars, and the miners lost about twenty-five million dollars in wages.

Following the strike victory, the United Mine Workers became the largest and most powerful labor union in the United States. President Roosevelt's intervention led to the establishment of the Federal Government as a mediator between powerful groups in society.

More than 10,000 immigrants went back to their homeland, as they could not withstand the length of the strike. Without any steady wages, many found it hard to keep their lodging rent up-to-date and were forced out of their rooms and apartments.

Because of the vacancies in small apartments in Pittston, Pennsylvania, Frank Policare was able to move to South Main Street, Pittston. He sent a letter to Anna with money for her passage to come to America. Many of the Italian immigrants who arrived in Pittston chose to live near each other in the Oregon Section, Railroad and Pine Streets, or South Main Street.

*Chapter 3*

## MARRIAGE AND JOURNEY TO NAPLES, ITALY

In Italy Michael and Rosa (Jannare) Policare lived a few miles from the Romano family. They had a large family, and many traveled to the United States of America. Because of their crowded living conditions, it was an easy decision to make. Some family members wrote that they stayed in New York City to work on the roads and the subway. Many traveled to Pittston, Pennsylvania, where family members worked in the coal mines.

Carl Romano and Rocco Policare, good friends, stopped to talk outside the church on a Sunday morning. Carl's sister Maria, accompanied by her family, came out of the church. Rocco was seven years older than Maria, who just turned eighteen. He was immediately attracted by her beauty and sweet smile. Maria was a very pretty young woman. Rocco approached her with a warm greeting and a smile. Because of the age difference, he didn't have much interaction with her previously. After talking to her for a short period of time, he asked Carl if he would ask her father's permission to visit his family on Sunday afternoon. Carl asked his father, and Mr. Carlo Romano said he was welcome to visit.

Rocco, tall and slender with straight dark hair and brown eyes, had a big smile and a jovial personality. He was always calm and friendly. In the afternoon, Rocco visited with the Romano family. He took a walk with Maria and asked her what she would want in her future. Maria replied that she would want to have many children. Maria was tall with a curvy build and delicate features with high cheekbones and a light complexion. Her long, brown wavy hair had red highlights. Her teeth were exceptionally white and straight. Her lips were dark pink as though they had red rouge on them. Her brown eyes were beautiful and seductive. That day she wore a plain blue dress made by her mother. After a two-month courtship, Rocco asked her father for Maria's hand in marriage. Carlo Romano granted his permission for Rocco to marry Maria.

On a beautiful sunny day, Rocco and Maria went for a walk by a stream. There are many varieties of wild flowers growing in southern Italy. Rocco collected a small bouquet of wild peonies and roses, making a bouquet for Maria. There was a large rock near the stream, and Maria and Rocco rested there for a moment. At that point, Rocco picked up the bouquet and gave it to Maria. Kneeling on one knee, Rocco asked Maria if she would be his wife. Smiling and overjoyed, Maria said yes. After sharing their good news with their families, they met the next day with Father Giovanni to arrange their marriage.

They were married on March 2nd, 1901 at St. Mary's church in Calimera, Italy. Before Anna left for the United States of America, she was matron of honor for her sister. Carl Romano was best man for Rocco.

The altar was adorned with wild flowers, and the candles were lit on each side of the altar. There were small candles glowing in the high windows on each side of the church. Cousin Joseph Romano was playing the violin softly.

Carlo Romano proudly held his daughter's arm as he walked her down the aisle. The pews of the church were filled with family and friends from the town. Father Giovanni, Carl Romano, and Rocco Policare watched as she came down the aisle. Rocco, dressed in a white shirt and tie and black pants, waited expectantly and joyfully for his beautiful bride.

Victoria Romano made a delicate full-length linen dress for Maria. It had a scoop neckline adorned with small crocheted pink roses. Her hair was pulled back in a long braid. Interwoven in the braid was a pink ribbon; at the end, it had a delicate bow. She wore a small shoulder length veil surrounding a circle of fresh baby pink roses. She carried a small bouquet of multi-color wild flowers surrounded by greens and tied with a pink ribbon. Before she walked down the aisle, her mother removed her gold crucifix necklace and put it on Maria. She had worn it for thirty years and now it was to be her gift to Maria. As Maria walked down the aisle, she smiled at Rocco as he waited for her at the altar. Carlo Romano gave his daughter's hand to Rocco and returned to the pew to sit with Victoria. The Mass was welcoming, and Father Giovanni led them in exchanging their vows. Rocco had a small, thin gold ring to place on Maria's finger. When the Mass was over, they turned and walked down the aisle. They waited at the entrance of the church to be greeted by their family and friends. On the porch of the church were two large hearts drawn with chalk and filled with rice. This is a good luck custom in Italy. Everyone followed them from the church.

The Policare and Romano families walked behind the newly married couple to the home of her mother and father. They were happy and singing with accompaniment from Joseph Romano playing the violin and Francesco Aruzzo playing the harmonica.

When they arrived home, everything was in place for a family dinner. They put two tables together, so everyone could sit at one large table. The two families took their seats, and Carl Romano stood and gave a wine toast to his sister and best friend, "I wish Rocco and Maria a long marriage and many children."

In the center of the table was a vase filled with wild flowers collected in the open fields by Maria's mother. The women served the meal of homemade pasta with fish and vegetables covered with marinara sauce. There were two baskets of freshly made bread. After the meal, everyone danced to the music.

After the joyful festivities, Victoria went into the house to get dessert. Penalattis are very popular in the Italian culture as a perfect end to a meal. They are small dough balls fried in olive oil and dipped in honey. Maria's mother shaped them into a mound, and Maria and Rocco put them in small plates for the guests to eat. Afterwards, when everyone was finished dancing, they served Zeppolis with wine. Zeppolis are fried dough with raisins coated with sugar.

When the wedding feast ended, Maria and Rocco walked to the two-room cottage owned by their cousin Dominic Paglianite. Dominic and his family left Italy and traveled to Argentina to work. Maria and Rocco prepared the cottage to live in until they would leave for America. On the morning of their marriage, Rocco picked flowers and put them in a vase to surprise Maria. This time when they arrived at the cottage, Rocco and Maria were married and he carried her over the threshold. They were very happy and laughing as they entered the cottage. Maria thought to herself, I hope we could be this happy forever.

Rocco lit one candle for some light. At that point, Maria could see the pretty flowers placed on the table for her. As he kissed her and removed the ribbon from her hair, Maria's hair fell to her shoulders in wavy curls. As they undressed, Maria was very shy. He kissed her and caressed her neck. Her dress fell to the floor and her stomach fluttered. Rocco had never kissed her like this before. He touched her gently as they lay on the bed. She sighed with delight as they consummated their marriage. It was perfect, they were in love. The next morning, they made love again.

The following day, on the way to the fields to work, they stopped to say goodbye to Anna. She was going to Rosarno, Italy to take the train to Naples, Italy. She would then board the boat to the United States of America to be with her husband Frank. She was accompanied by other cousins traveling to New York City, New York.

The following month, Maria realized she was pregnant with their first child. Everyone in the family was very happy for them and awaited the birth. She still worked, side by side, with Rocco in the fields picking vegetables. Rocco did double work, so Maria would have an easier workday. As her due date neared, she remained in the cottage to rest. Her parents and other family members stayed with her while Rocco went to work in the fields.

On January 2nd, 1902, Rocco went to tell Victoria and Carlo that Maria was in labor. They notified the doctor and they then gathered at the cottage while Maria experienced labor pains every half hour. As they waited through the night, the pains became more frequent. Close to midnight on January 2nd, 1902, as Maria was moaning in pain, their first child, Rosa, came into the world.

Rosa was a delicate, small baby girl with curly black hair and olive skin. As she cried at birth, her dark brown eyes opened, but she soon fell asleep in the arms of her mother and father. When she awoke again, she started to cry, and Maria nursed her baby, which came naturally to her.

After Rosa was born, Carlo and Victoria stayed with Rocco and Maria until she was able to care for Rosa by herself. After Maria was well and able to care for Rosa, her parents said goodbye to Rocco and Maria. Carlo and Victoria sailed from Naples, Italy in the steerage compartment of the ship, to New York City. After processing at Ellis Island, they boarded a train to Pittston, Pennsylvania. They would stay with Frank and Anna until they could settle in a place of their own. Carlo was able to find work in Pittston with his brother Joseph, who had a large vegetable garden and fruit trees. He sold his fruit and vegetables to neighbors. Many Italians would have fruit and vegetable gardens to provide food for their families. At night he went to work in the coal mines.

Within a few months, Maria was pregnant again. In the beginning of 1903, Rocco and Maria welcomed their second baby, Michael, into their loving and growing family. With dark hair, dark eyes, olive skin, and a beautiful smile, Michael looked like Rocco.

After saving for their trip to America and receiving money from Maria's father, Rocco and Maria started to plan their trip to Rosarno, Italy, where they would board the train to Naples. The trip would take approximately two hours, and they planned to board the ship in early 1903. They left their cottage in perfect condition for the next family couple that needed it. They packed what they thought would be needed for the trip on the ship. Previously Maria and her mother made two material suitcases for them to carry their belongings. They had a homemade blankets and booties for Rosa and Michael. He would be two-months-old when they were traveling by ship to the United States of America. They packed their clothing in each suitcase and some space was used for canned fruit and vegetables, grapes, raisins, cheese, bread, and water. Although their ticket for the ship included soup or stew each day, they wanted to take some of their own food. Hopefully they will be allowed to take it on board.

In Calabria, Italy, the terrain was uneven and hilly, the roads were not paved, and many families did not have their own horse or burrow for transportation. On March 12th, 1903, Rocco and Maria made plans with Joseph Ranieli to travel with his wagon and burrow to the train station in Rosarno, Italy. As they started to leave Calimera and come down from the hills, Rocco asked Joseph to pause the wagon.

He said, "Maria, let's turn around and look at the hills of Calabria, we want to keep their image in our minds, we may never see them again." Maria and Rocco looked back with tears in their eyes.

This was their homeland. They were born and reared in Italy. They didn't know their future but knew they had to make the journey. It was a chance to have a better life for them and future generations.

It would take two hours to travel from the hills and go through the few towns along the way. As they passed through San Cologio, they waved to family and friends. Their friend Gregorio (Billy) Paglianite went over to the wagon and wished them well. He was also saving for his trip to America. The town of San Cologio was becoming empty like other towns in southern Italy with many vacancies in the apartments. Because of the deteriorating living conditions, there was no choice but to travel to the United States or Argentina.

Two hours later, Rocco and Maria, carrying Rosa and Michael, arrived in Rosarno, Italy to board the train to Naples. This is the first time Rocco and Maria were on a train amongst a large crowd of passengers. They could understand most of the dialects of the southern region of Italy. There were older passengers and families with many children. Their destination was the same. They were traveling to Naples, Italy to board the ships to the United States of America. Some were there previously and came home to see their families. They provided money earned to rebuild their town in Italy. Many had plans to return to Italy, and a great number accomplished this wish. They would live in boarding houses, work in the mines and other industries, and earn enough money to return to Italy and help their families.

Arriving at Naples, Italy, Rocco and Maria could see the pier and ships that were to sail the following day. They stayed in the terminal to wait for departure. As they stood in line to show the ticket agent their prepaid ticket, a doctor came to question them about their health. He asked them a few basic questions and then proceeded to the next person in line. After the previous passengers disembarked, the facilities were cleaned and sprayed. There was a smell of the chemical used. Before they walked up the gangplank to board the ship, they and their luggage were sprayed with disinfectant.

After the disinfectant dried, they walked up the gangplank to board the ship. There were ship workers checking their papers and inspecting their luggage contents. The young man looked at them with a smile and did not remove their food from the luggage.

There were three levels of passengers on the ship, first class, second class, and steerage. Their tickets were for the steerage area. They had to go down two flights of steps and walk by the steering and engine compartments into the steerage area. At first they were very alarmed because it was dark and dreary and had recently been sprayed with disinfectant.

Each passenger and family were given a bunk area for their voyage. It was approximately seven feet long by six feet high. There was a straw mattress and a pillow. There was another area above them and another family was assigned this area. There were three different compartments in the steerage area, single men, single women, and families. They were in the family area. There wasn't much room, and passengers were sitting in close proximity to each other. Rocco and Maria had enough room to sit and a small area for Rosa and Michael to sleep. At night they were able to lie down with the children between them. Their luggage was at their feet. Even though the accommodations were not good, they knew in a week or two they would be in America. All the children walked around and greeted each other. There were separate washing facilities for the women and men. The workers on the ship were friendly and came down to talk to the families in steerage. They answered a few questions and exited the area. Soon the engines were started and the ship left the dock. They were on their way to start a new life in the United States of America.

At meal time, the crew came down to the steerage area and handed out a tin with eating utensils for everyone. They would have to clean them and use them for the whole trip. There wasn't a dining area, and most passengers stood to eat their food. Rocco waited in line to get the stew provided at dinner time while Maria stayed with Rosa and Michael. Tonight's meal was potato and vegetable stew with a small amount of meat. The poor grade of meat was hard to chew. When some of the passengers complained and could not eat it, the crewman explained this is the soup they would receive with the steerage ticket. As they finished their meal, they could hear loud talking and laughing coming from the other areas in steerage.

After a few hours, the children quieted down and everyone went to sleep. Rosa and Michael liked the rocking of the ship and never cried. The next morning came quickly. The crew came down to give them their breakfast. They had milk for the children and gave two cups to Maria because she had a small child and an infant. Rocco stood in line to get their breakfast, which consisted of mushy cereal. They were not used to this in Italy but ate what was provided. They also had coffee and tea for everyone. The bathrooms were in use throughout the day and night. There were approximately 100 people in their compartment. After a few days went by, they were allowed, twenty people at a time, to go to the small deck near the steerage entrance. It was good to get the fresh air and look at the ocean.

Above them they could see the passengers in first and second class. They looked down at them in surprise and disbelief, as though they didn't know there were people below them in steerage. Passengers from the different areas and classes rarely saw each other. They came from different worlds, and the people in steerage could only dream that someday they would have better clothes and take the ship again to Italy in first or second class.

Every day was the same with long lines for food and the bathrooms. As the week drew to a close, the crew came to tell them they were going through rough seas and a storm was on the horizon. Not knowing what to expect, everyone was frightened. By night, as the boat swayed back and forth, the children fell on the floor. Rocco and Maria stayed in their area and put Rosa and Michael under their blanket and held them tightly next to them. With the rocking of the ship, everyone was afraid of what was to come. Hopefully the ship was large enough to withstand the wind and the high waves. People were getting sea sick and vomiting on the floor. By the next morning, the storm ended. The crew came down the stairs and said they could go on deck for some fresh air. Their compartment smelled terrible, and people moaned in their bunks.

Rocco and Maria went on deck with the children. It was good to breathe the fresh air. Although the storm was over, the waves were still high. They could see pieces of wood in the water and wondered if another small boat had been torn apart. Although storms come up quickly in the ocean, everyone hoped this would be the only one.

As the second week passed, everyone was anxious to land at Ellis Island, New York. Everything smelled terrible in steerage and it was to the point people did not want to eat anything. The food Rocco and Maria packed was gone, and they had to eat what was given to them.

Always playing, dancing, and singing, the children adjusted to the trip much better than the adults. To pass time, a Greek woman told fortunes, but Maria wasn't interested in asking about her future.

After two weeks, the ship was coming close to landing in America. Finally, when the crew announced they would be able to see the torch on the top of the Statue of Liberty, the women decided to find some blue and red cloth from their clothing to make little flags to wave. As they neared the Statue, the passengers were so excited, no one wanted to sleep. Some stayed up all night.

The next morning, everyone was on deck. Soon someone yelled in Italian they could see the top of the torch! The crew told them it would take a few hours to get close enough to see the whole statue. Other ships were coming in at the same time; it was a beautiful sight.

Soon as the passengers saw the Statue of Liberty, everyone was crying and waving their little red and blue homemade flags. As they came close, the crewman yelled in Italian, "GIVE ME YOUR TIRED, YOUR POOR, YOUR HUDDLED MASSES YEARNING TO BREATHE FREE, THE WRETCHED REFUSE OF YOUR TEEMING SHORE. SEND THESE, THE HOMELESS, TEMPEST-TOST TO ME, I LIFT MY LAMP BESIDE THE GOLDEN DOOR."

Rocco looked at Maria and said, "We arrived in the United States of America and we are welcome."

*FIGURE 1. STATUE OF LIBERTY*

*FIGURE 2. ELLIS ISLAND*

# Chapter 4

## ELLIS ISLAND

The Ellis Island Immigrant Inspection Station opened on January 1st, 1892. The station's main building was constructed of Georgia pine and measuring 404 feet long, 154 feet wide, and three stories high with turrets on each side. It could accommodate twice as many inspectors as the previous Castle Garden Center.

A ferry pulled up alongside the "Nevada." Annie Moore, her two brothers, and other steerage passengers climbed aboard while sailors brought the immigrants trunks, bags, and bundles on to the ferry. The reason their transport was so festively decorated soon spread among the passengers of the three ships that had spent the night anchored in New York harbor. Theirs had been chosen to be the first processed at New York's new immigrant landing station. Little Annie Moore, "a rosy cheeked Irish girl," walked down the ramp first. Her name was recorded in the history of Ellis Island. The immigrants would store their luggage, buy food and train tickets, and undergo medical inspections on the first floor and then proceed to the second floor for questioning and registration by immigration inspectors. As many as 15,000 immigrants per day were processed.

With thousands of people passing through the wooden structure each day, the building could not possibly last very long. Shortly after midnight on June 15th, 1897, a huge fire destroyed the massive wooden building and virtually everything else on Ellis Island. All records from 1855, through the time of fire, were lost.

Congress appropriated sufficient funds to build a more impressive and durable structure. The legislators also allocated money to increase the size of the island to seventeen acres, so that additional buildings could be constructed. The Treasury Department quickly organized an architectural competition for the new buildings, and the winners were a pair of young architects, William Boring and Edward Lippincott Tilton.

The main building was almost precisely the same size as the one it replaced and was laid out almost identically with baggage, food, transfers being handled on the first floor, inspections and registration on the second floor, and administrative offices and a gallery overlooking the inspection area on the third level, capped with towers at each corner of the structure. The exterior, with its mixture of classical and French and Italian motifs, exemplified the Beaux-Arts style, named for the art school in Paris where both Boring and Tilton had studied architecture.

The inspection of immigrants in the new station began on December 17th, 1900. Ellis Island was the gateway for twelve million immigrants who came to the United States from 1892 until 1954. The iconic brick and limestone building still stands today.

As Maria and Rocco and the children were on deck with the other steerage passengers, processing began with the first and second-class passengers. First and second-class passengers were not required to undergo the inspection process at Ellis Island. They underwent cursory inspections aboard ship. The theory was that if people could afford to purchase a first or second-class ticket, they were less likely to become a public charge in America due to medical or legal reasons. The government felt these more affluent passengers would not end up in institutions or hospitals. They would not become a burden of the state. First and second-class passengers would disembark, pass through Customs at the pier, and then they were free to enter the United States. Only those determined to be sick or having legal problems were sent to Ellis Island for further inspection.

After processing the first and second-class passengers, the crewmen would call out the names of the steerage passengers and have each one step forward to pin a large piece of paper to the person's clothing with a letter and a number on it. Rocco and Maria's names were called and they were given numbers and letters to place on their clothing. The same numbers and letters were attached to their bags. It listed the name of the steamship, manifest sheet, and passenger number. Finally everyone was told to get on the barge for their short trip to

Ellis Island. It was very cramped, cold, and unsteady because of the waves. Because there were other barges loaded with passengers, they had to wait for their turn to land at Ellis Island. Due to the long wait, most of the children were crying. As they waited to land, some of the sick children died because of the cold temperatures on the barges or ferries. If the inspectors' workday ended before all the immigrants could be processed, immigrant passengers would be brought back to the ship to spend another night. Many times the inspectors would work overtime until everyone transported to Ellis Island that day had been processed.

After waiting a few hours in the freezing cold, it was Rocco and Maria's turn to disembark from the barge. With the help of the dockworkers, Rocco and Maria, carrying Rosa and Michael, stepped onto the land. They held each other with the children between them and cried with joy. They arrived in America safely and now had to go through processing. In the distance, they could see the large buildings of New York City. They were in awe of the clusters of buildings, some higher than others, that formed the New York City skyline.

The lines were long, but it didn't matter because everyone was excited, anxious, and apprehensive. The immigrants waited many hours because numerous ships arrived at the same time. As Rocco and Maria entered the building, they could see the railings that guided their path through the registry room. Soon it was their turn to talk to the processing officials with their roster and ticket information. The baggage room was on the left. Many had large trunks and they were given to the baggage agents for processing.

Rocco and Maria had two pieces of baggage and kept them by their side. At the right and left of the room, there were telegraph offices and a railroad ticket agent. It was very noisy with many different languages being spoken.

*FIGURE 3. MAIN FLOOR ELLIS ISLAND- COURTESY OF NEW YORK PUBLIC LIBRARY AND ELLIS ISLAND*

After processing on the main floor, Rocco and Maria went up the center staircase to the Great Hall for further inspection. The second floor had a circular balcony enclosed by a railing, and on each side there were different rooms for processing the immigrants. As the immigrants walked up the steps, the doctors viewed them from above to watch for weakness, heavy breathing, and signs of mental disturbances. When every immigrant passed, the doctor, with the help of an interpreter, examined hair, face, neck, and hands of every person. The very kind interpreters tried their best to help the immigrants.

The doctor had a chalk in his hand; when he noticed that some area needed to be checked more thoroughly, he wrote a letter on the immigrant's clothes. This check became known as the six second check. About two out of ten persons got a letter on their clothes. The meaning of the letters was: X-high up at the frontside of right shoulder—mental defects. X- further down on the right shoulder—disease or deformity. X—within a circle—some definite disease. B—back problems. G—struma. H—heart problems. PG—pregnancy. CT—eye disease. If they had a letter marked on their lapel, they would go into another line for further examination. Immigrants who did not pass the physical would be sent to the hospital to hopefully recover from their illnesses.

Soon the immigrants reached a second doctor, the "eye man." He stood with his back to a window, so that he could use the natural light to examine immigrants' eyes. First, he looked directly into each eye for signs of opaque corneas or other common eye diseases. Then, using either his thumb and forefinger or a buttonhook-like material instrument, the doctor would pull the immigrant's upper eyelid away from the face to look for signs of conjunctivitis or trachoma, a bacterial infection of the eye whose telltale symptom was roughening of the inner eyelid. This disease rendered an immigrant ineligible to enter the United States.

Due to desire to process the immigrants as quickly as possible, Ellis Island eye doctors did not typically bother to wash their hands or clean their instruments between the examination of successive immigrants.

President Theodore Roosevelt complained to his Secretary of Commerce and Labor, Victor Metcalf, after touring Ellis Island in 1906, "I was stuck by the way in which the doctors made the (trachoma) examinations with dirty hands and with no pretense to clean the instruments. It would seem to me that these examinations as conducted would themselves be a fruitful source of carrying infection from diseased to healthy people."

Nearly eighty percent of the immigrants denied entry to the United States for medical reasons suffered from trachoma. "When they learned their fate, they were stunned," recalled Fiorello LaGuardia, who worked as an interpreter at Ellis Island before he entered politics. "They had never felt ill. They had never heard the word trachoma. They could see all right." Worst of all, LaGuardia wrote, were the cases in which a family had sold virtually everything it owned to come to America. "If in that family a young child were suffering from trachoma, one of the parents had to return to the native country with the rejected member of the family."

But because of the potential for trachoma to spread, especially from child to child during play, inspectors considered its discovery a cause for mandatory exclusion. Only in 1919, Congress passed a law requiring trachoma examinations at ports of embarkation.

As Rocco, Maria, and the children were waiting in line, the gentleman in front of them had a letter put on his lapel. Being very upset, he talked in a loud voice in his native language. At that point, an interpreter and a guard came forward to speak to him. It was a frightening experience because no one knew what would happen if they couldn't enter the United States.

After the man was taken out of the line, it was Maria, Rocco, and the children's turn to be given their physicals. The women would have to go into a room with a female nurse and doctor. Many single women were embarrassed because they were not given a physical exam by a doctor in their native land. If there were problems with their paperwork or some other reason to detain immigrants at Ellis Island, they were put in the Detention Room. This room was located on the right side of the second floor.

There were three rows of beds with two beds side by side stacked. They were provided a blanket and a pillow. There was running water in the room to drink. They would be scheduled for a hearing of their case on the third floor of Ellis Island.

*FIGURE 4. DETENTION ROOM AT ELLIS ISLAND (COURTESY ELLIS ISLAND)*

After Maria and Rocco and the children passed their physicals, they proceeded to the dining room located on the right of the first floor where immigrants could buy food when they entered or left Ellis Island. The dining room was large with dark mahogany wood tables and chairs. There were beautiful brightly colored murals on the walls, which made for a very pleasant and welcoming atmosphere. The menu had many different items that reflected foods eaten by immigrants from different parts of the world.

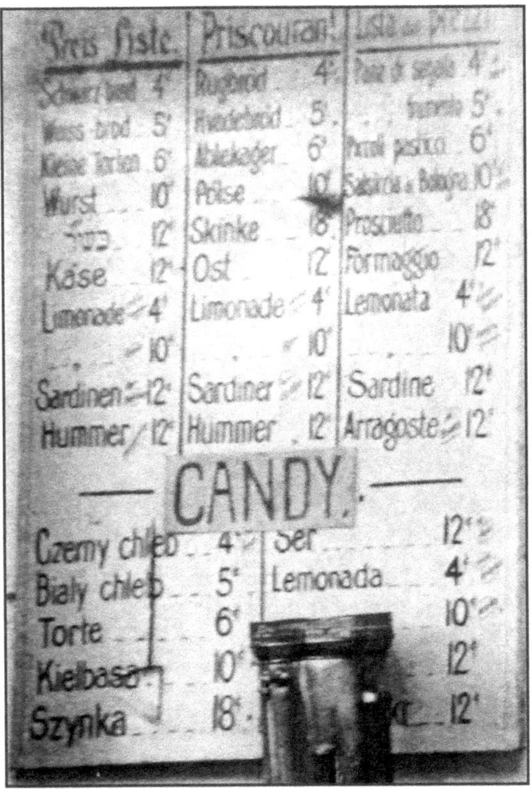

FIGURE 5. ORIGINAL MENU POSTED AT ELLIS ISLAND (COURTESY ELLIS ISLAND)

In the dining area, a man dressed in white pushing a cart rang a bell. He would come around every morning and afternoon. He would blow a whistle and all the kids would line up. He would give each child a small paper cup and pour some milk from a stainless-steel pitcher into each cup. If immigrants entered Ellis Island in the morning, they received oatmeal with a little bit of sugar on top. Many immigrants were not familiar with this food and could not eat it.

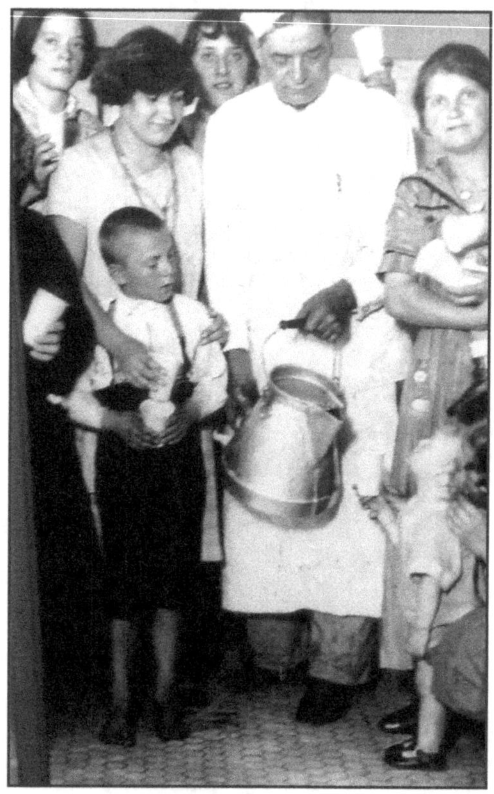

FIGURE 6. MAN SERVING CHILDREN MILK AT ELLIS ISLAND (COURTESY ELLIS ISLAND)

Most immigrants were processed and allowed into the country. Those who were thought to be sick or disabled, around one million in total, were sent to the massive hospital complex on the island's southside. There is a "Y" corridor that leads to the hospital complex. One hallway leads to the island hospital, built to restore the health of people suffering minor injuries, broken bones. Also, 350 babies were born at Ellis Island. The other hallway took patients to the Contagious and Infectious Disease Hospital where they were treated for deadly diseases, like diphtheria, scarlet fever, measles, and whooping cough. If an immigrant survived diphtheria, he or she would return to the immigration process. It was the people suffering from less serious conditions, maybe a broken knee or bad back, who would be sent home because they couldn't work. Initially the contagious and infectious hospital were separated from the main island hospital by a strip of water. Back then it was wrongly believed that germs couldn't travel across water. The water was eventually filled in with a grassy area where patients could stroll and get sunshine.

The complex had isolation wards. There were twelve patients to a room. The sick immigrants, along with the nursing staff, could be sealed in for weeks. The kitchen in the hospital complex cooked 1,500 meals a day. The hospital laundry room cleaned 3,000 pieces of hospital linens a day in giant washing machines, but keeping mattresses clean was another challenge.

A machine called the "mattress autoclave" steam-cleaned mattresses to kill bacteria. Approximately 3,500 people died at Ellis Island, but fortunately no staff members contracted diseases from their patients.

Maria and Rocco proceeded to the inspector's desk at the far end of the registry room for their legal examination, an experience that many compared to "the final day of judgement" to determine an immigrant's economic and moral fitness. Inspectors asked a series of questions, such as, "Are you married or single? Have you ever been convicted of a crime?" The interrogation was over in a matter of minutes, after which an immigrant was either permitted to enter the United States or detained for a legal hearing in front of the Board of Inquiry. At the inquiry, friends and relatives of the immigrants could provide testimony. Immigrants could testify on their own behalf. After hearing the evidence, the Board granted admission to most immigrants.

Rocco and Maria were very happy they were allowed to enter the United States of America. Their dreams would become a reality in the small mining town of Pittston, Pennsylvania. They went down the steps to get in line to buy their railroad tickets. The ticket agents were able to decide which trains they were to take to get to their destination by looking at the city and state listed on their paperwork.

Rocco went to purchase the tickets, and Maria was waiting for him with Rosa and Michael in her arms. The Greek woman on the ship came over to talk to her. She was also permitted to enter the United States of America.

As she looked at Maria and the children, she said, "Maria, you will have many children, but you will have a hard struggle in America." Maria turned away and did not respond. She did not want to hear her clairvoyant rant, but later she wondered why she didn't mention Rocco.

After immigrants had arranged their travel plans, they received boldly printed tags to put on their hats or coats. The tags showed railroad conductors what lines immigrants were traveling and what connections they would have to make to reach their destinations.

Ellis Island was called the "Isle of Hope – Isle of Tears." There were many different immigrants from different countries entering Ellis Island. The anxiety of being deported caused a chaotic mixture from fright and despair to joy and relief. For the ninety-eight percent who were permitted to land in the United States, Ellis Island was an "Isle of Hope." For the unfortunate two percent of the arrivals who were excluded and sent back to their points of embarkations, Ellis Island was a bitter "Isle of Tears." Though two percent may sound insignificant it translated into over 1,000 exclusions a month.

Only one third of the immigrants who came through Ellis Island stayed in New York City. The majority scattered to points all across the country in a railroad network that crisscrossed the entire continent and offered easy access to all of America's major cities.

Unaccompanied women and children were not allowed to go into New York City alone. There were a few organizations, such as The Immigrant Home for Girls, Women's Home, and the Methodist Church willing to provide for them until their families came to meet them. Everyday a Catholic priest from the local church would be there with money and information for shelter for men, women, and their children.

After Ellis Island closed in 1954, the interior walls gradually shed their many layers of paint, revealing surfaces covered with signatures, inscriptions, and drawings, visible evidence of the island's past left by the people who traveled through the place decades ago. During the 1980's restoration, conservators salvaged and preserved many of the graffiti. Examples are still preserved on some of the walls and windowsills in the detention room and various dormitories.

*Chapter 5*

## ARRIVAL IN PITTSTON, PENNSYLVANIA — 1903

After processing at Ellis Island, the newly arrived immigrants exited down the "Stairs of Separation." The stairs to the right led to rail stations for immediate passage to various cities and the stairs to the left led to the ferryboats to New York City. Many were going to New York City, whether or not they had a job waiting. People felt there was more opportunity in a large city.

Maria and Rocco Policare and their children were put on a ferry to Jersey City, New Jersey to board the Lehigh Valley Railroad train to Pittston, Pennsylvania. Due to the cold weather in January, they layered their clothes. When Michael cried, Maria nursed him and held him close to her body until they arrived at the train. Upon boarding they were relieved to see so many travelers from their boat going to the same destination, Pittston Pennsylvania. Most would be working in the anthracite coal mines.

The train had many cars to accommodate the passengers waiting to board. The engine car was blue with a flag on top, with the letters L and V. The passenger cars were grey and provided ample room for everyone. Rocco, Maria, and the children boarded the train and took their assigned seats. As the train left, everyone started to clap. Someone started to play a harmonica and everyone sang. Although they didn't know their future, they looked forward to a new life in America. Many came before them and after them, they arrived from many different countries to populate the United States of America. As they passed by towns along the way, people waved to them. It was a nice welcoming gesture.

Approximately four hours later, they arrived at the Wilkes-Barre, Pennsylvania train station. The Lehigh Valley passenger station, which was on the northeast side of Parrish Street, near South Main Street. The train was there long enough to let passengers off and allow others to board. Wilkes-Barre was a large city in the center of the Wyoming Valley anthracite coal region. It was founded in 1769 by John Durke and colonists from Connecticut and was originally known as Wyoming. Later it was renamed in honor of two British members of Parliament, John Wilkes and Col. Isaac Barre, who had defended the American colonies in parliamentary debates. In 1818 Wilkes-Barre was incorporated as a borough, with a city charter following in 1871.

Coal mining was not the only segment of the Wilkes-Barre economy. Charles Stegmaier began brewing beer in 1857, and by 1916, was producing 200,000 barrels a year. Silk manufacturing became important with companies, such as Empire Silk Mill, importing silk from Japan to be fashioned into women's garments.

Along the way, it was interesting to see the mining communities with small, dark, one or two room shanties or shacks in a row. These were called patch towns where the coal miners lived close to the mines where they worked. Gradually they grew into a community with a variety of housing types, including boarding houses for transients and new hires, the growing community organized around a company store. The mine owners owned the company stores and expected their workers to buy all their goods from them. Frequently all of their paychecks were owed to the company store for purchases "on the book," and workers were left with little money for the rest of the month. Many of the goods offered were at higher prices than other stores, but the miners were forced to purchase all goods from the company store.

On their way to Pittston, Maria and Rocco passed by other mining towns. They saw the large, dark grey coal breakers dotting the landscape. They were hundreds of feet high in the air and had different shaped areas butting out from under the main roof. The coal would be crushed into various size pieces each with a different burning capacity. There were windows in each area covered with soot and dirt.

The train traveled on the tracks alongside the Susquehanna River for approximately thirty minutes. Although it was a beautiful sunny day with a light blue sky, it was cold. Many trees and shrubs covered the mountains and the river banks. Snow and icicles hung from the limbs. Patches of solid ice covered with snow flowed on the river. Little sparkles of silver in the snow was reflected from the sunlight. This was the first time the Italian immigrants saw snow, and it was one of the most beautiful sights.

Pittston is midway between Wilkes-Barre and Scranton. Scranton is located in the heart of one of the great deposits of anthracite coal in the world. Mining provided the underpinnings for much of Scranton's industries until the middle of the 20th century. It is the largest of the anthracite mining communities in a contiguous quilt-work that also includes Wilkes-Barre, Pittston, and Carbondale. In 1845 the name given to the settlement was Harrison in honor of the president of the United States. Finally, in 1851, the name was changed to Scranton after George and Seldon Scranton. In 1840 the Scranton brothers built a forge that later became the nucleus of the Lackawanna Iron and Steel Company.

Pittston was incorporated as a borough on April 30th,1853 and incorporated as a city on December 10th, 1894. The city's area is 1.7 square miles. It gained prominence in the late 19th and early 20th centuries as an active coal mining city, drawing a large portion of its labor force from European immigrants. The city consists of three sections: The Downtown (in the center of the city), the Oregon Section (in the southern end), and the Junction (in the northern end). It lay in the Wyoming Valley on the east side of the Susquehanna River and on the south side of the Lackawanna River. The anthracite and railroad industry attracted thousands of immigrants, making Pittston a true melting pot with once-distinct ethnic and class neighborhoods.

'As the train approached Pittston and neared the Lehigh Valley Train Station, it slowed down. The first thing Maria noticed were the beautiful, high church steeples of Saint John the Evangelist Church, The First Presbyterian Church, The Methodist Church, and Saint James Episcopal Church.

She said to Rocco, "We are in the right place, this is a religious community."

As the train slowed, they could see the Lehigh Valley Railroad train station at 30 Water Street. This beautiful, state-of-the art station opened on May 20th, 1896. It replaced a sparse wooden structure near the same site. The station was a brick building with quarried stone trimmings. The lower floor, on level with the railroad tracks, was for passenger service and contained the waiting rooms, baggage rooms, and a boarding pavilion. A broad stairway led to the second-floor ticket office. The second floor was level with Water Street. A brick driveway was built for carriages and baggage wagons to have access to the lower floor. The interior plaster had a blush sand finish trimmed with ash woodwork. The waiting rooms were richly furnished and had three brick fireplaces. The large windows in the ladies waiting room gave a view of the river. The building had electric wiring and gas pipes. On top of the green roof was a clock tower. On top of the tower was a weather vane.

As the train stopped, the passengers saw a large group of people waiting for their arrival. They were waving American flags and smiling. Seeing their family in the crowd, Rocco and Maria hurried to leave the train. Maria's parents Carlo and Victoria Romano waited with mittens and coats for them. When Rocco and Maria, carrying Rosa and Michael, left the train, everyone hugged and kissed and were happy they arrived safely. Carlo and Victoria were surprised at how much Rosa grew from the last time they saw her and were thrilled to meet their second grandchild Michael.

Maria and Rocco were anxious to explore the City of Pittston. After going upstairs in the beautiful train station, they walked onto the sidewalk. Horse and buggy carriages clomped up and down the dirt streets.

As they reached the corner, there was a large sign Sutherland and McMillian Columbia Flour. Sutherland and McMillan was a grocery distributor located in a large building behind the First Baptist Church.

*FIGURE 7. TOWER OF TRAIN STATION, TOLL BRIDGE, POST OFFICE ON WATER STREET (COURTESY GREATER PITTSTON HISTORICAL SOCIETY)*

A light snow was falling, and Maria held out her hand to feel it. She was amazed at how the snowflake would disappear as it rested on her hand. Because of the cold weather, they hurried to put on the mittens and cover themselves with the coats made by her mother.

As they walked up Water Street, they noticed a large cross on top of the First Baptist Church located at 20 Water Street. It was a two-story cement and brick church with stained glass windows and a large porch. Surrounded by a wooden fence, it was founded in 1776; it is the oldest church in Pittston. Church records indicate Baptist gospel services in Pittston as early 1769. It was built in 1776, the year the original thirteen colonies united as a new nation. The Reverend Ebenezer West of Wyoming Valley and the Reverend James Benedict of Warwick, New York officially organized a small congregation as First Baptist Church of Pittston. Just two years later, in 1778, the church nearly folded when several members either died in or were dispersed by the Battle of Wyoming, often called the Wyoming Massacre. Even though only twelve members remained, they survived as an organization. The 240th anniversary of the founding of the church was held on September 25th, 2015.

Pittston City Hall was close by at 14 Water Street. All city business was conducted in this building. Next to City Hall was the Pittston City jail. The Niagara Engine Co. #2 was located at 10 Water Street. The Niagara Hose Company was organized July 27th, 1875. A year later, the company acquired its first steamer, purchased at the cost of $5,000. As Maria, Rocco, and the children continued on Water Street, some of the firemen were outside greeting the passengers from the train. Although they couldn't understand English, the friendly smiles from the firemen confirmed they were welcome. The Eagle Hose Company, the first in the city of Pittston, organized in 1857. Originally called Pittston Hose Company No. 1, the name was changed to Eagle in 1866. In 1857, the company had its quarters in a one-story brick structure on the present site.

Another story was added, and in 1913, the present building of three stories with social and living rooms and a modern gymnasium was constructed. In later years, the Niagara Hose Company joined with the Eagle Hose Company.

The Eagle Hose Company was famous for their fifteen-time State Championship Drill Team, and in September 1902, the Eagle Hose Company started a basketball team. By 1893 the Pittston YMCA had a team. By 1895, there was a local YMCA league of seven-man teams. Pittston won the championship, beating Scranton, Kingston and Wilkes-Barre. The Eagles players, having been part of the championship drill team, were disciplined, as well as big and athletic. Nanticoke was the Eagles' sacrificial lamb, in the first game on the third floor of the Kirby Block, corner of Main and Dock streets. The Eagles scored more points than any local team ever, winning 50-7. They played two or three times a week and continued to win big. They beat Carbondale 50-2. They also beat the Scranton Orientals, Bloomsburg State Normal, and Lafayette College. The Eagles didn't lose a game at Kirby Hall until March, and it took a professional team to beat them. Camden, leaders of the National League, beat the Eagles twice in Kirby Hall. Today, the Dime Bank Building is on the former site of Kirby Hall.

"Miss M. Emery's Hats and Bonnets" was located at 8 Water Street. As they passed, Maria looked at the beautiful hats on display in the window. The women's clothes in Pittston were quite fashionable with many clothing stores providing the latest fashions. In the same building was the "Singer Sewing Machine Company." This building was owned by James Corcoran. On the corner facing Main Street was a store occupied by "Lutz and Holleran Druggists" and "Burt Snowdon, Jeweler."

Archibald Miller, dentist, had his office at 1 Water Street, and the Postal Telegraph Company was at 3 Water Street. Mr. W.F. Staley, Pittston's leading jeweler, had his store at 5 Water Street. He was a watch inspector for the Erie and Lehigh Valley Railroads. Dr. Sanford Underwood opened his office at 7 Water Street. Dr. Underwood later became the Chief of Staff at the Pittston Hospital built in the Oregon Section of Pittston. "Ross and Company," sellers of eggs, cheese, and butter, sold their groceries at 15 Water Street. "Citizens Electric Illuminating Company" occupied 19 Water Street.

As Rocco and Maria walked to the opposite side of the Water Street, called Music Hall Block, they were amazed by the theater. Music Hall was built shortly after the Civil War. On September 17th, 1906, the name was changed to Lyric Theater, and at a later date, to Family Theater. This theater was owned by Harry D'Esta and Maurice Boon.

The owners brought first rate vaudeville acts to the city of Pittston. Outside of New York and Philadelphia, it was recognized as one of the finest opera houses in the country. It featured the outstanding actors and actresses and the most important Shakespearean performers of that period, including: Lily Langtry, Walter Scanlon, Chester De Vonde, Walter Mantell, Pat Rooney, and Emma Bunting.

The Post Office built at 21 Water Street included many different agencies and offices. Mr. William Peck was the Postmaster at the time. At 25 Water Street stood The Wyoming Valley Hotel, one of many hotels in Pittston. Boyles Saloon was a popular place in this hotel.

They could see the steeple of Saint James Episcopal Church on Charles Street. It was established in 1848 by three students from the Virginia Theological Seminary. The parish was organized in August 12th, 1849. The building, with a large steeple, was erected in 1858. The first reverend of the church was John Long in 1852. Because of mine subsidence, the church closed, and a large part of the congregation joined the Episcopal church in West Pittston.

There was a toll booth at the entrance of the Water Street Toll Bridge. The toll was one penny for pedestrians to walk across and twenty cents was charged for a two- horse team. The major force in the development of West Pittston was the West Pittston Land Association, which was formed in 1850. They purchased the Peter Rolin farm in 1851 and laid out the town into streets. They divided the land into lots for development. The lots sold quickly, and soon a thriving village had sprung up. On November 23rd, 1857, it was established as a borough. In 1859 the borough was encouraging planting of shade trees to enhance the beauty of the community. It was called "The Garden Village."

As it got colder, it was starting to snow again. The family walked to the corner of Main and Water streets. As they continued down South Main Street, they were in awe of the beautiful buildings. The four and five-story brick and cement buildings were from the Renaissance Revival Italianate period. Each had very decorative roof facade designs of flowers, faces, and fancy balconies with iron railings jutting out from the roof of the buildings. The windows were encased with cement leaf and circular designs. Also, there were many two and three-story buildings constructed of wood. All the buildings were connected and had roll out colorful awnings of different colors and designs. Many had large picture windows in front to display their merchandise. On the upper floors of the buildings, there were apartments for the incoming immigrants and offices for various companies. It was very exciting for Rocco and Maria to see the Main Street because they came from a very small town in southern Italy.

*FIGURE 8. MAIN STREET 1900 (COURTESY GREATER PITTSTON HISTORICAL SOCIETY)*

The sidewalks and street were very crowded with men, women, and children. Horse drawn wagons with passengers and supplies trotted along in both directions. Coal miners, who walked home from work after their shift, were covered with coal dust and their faces were black. Many stopped at the "Model Café" owned by John McHale at 10 South Main Street. W. A. Steinmeyer's Cigar Store was in the same building.

Thomas Schwartzkopf Liquors occupied 12 South Main Street while Mr. Joseph Reap, dentist, had his office at 13 South Main Street. Maria and Rocco were surprised to see Fitch-Nebone pianos and sheet music for sale at 14 ½ South Main. The Peoples Store, which sold dry goods and clothes, advertised that its basement was filled with holiday bargains and sold them at 15 South Main Street. The site of Postal Telegraph Cable Company was next door at 15 ½ South Main Street.

There were beautiful clothes in the store front window of Max Waldman established at 19 South Main Street. This building also housed Austin Sylvester Powers Plumbing and Heating. As Maria and Rocco walked by his store, Mr. Powers was removing large steel heating parts. Rocco stopped to help him load his wagon. He was grateful for the help and smiled at Rocco and shook his hand. Austin Powers was a large man with a beard and a big smile. He had piercing blue eyes and was proud of his Irish heritage. His plumbing and heating business was founded in 1892, two years before Pittston was incorporated as a city. He was a tradesman apprenticed to Sam Kresge, the famous department store magnet who was known as S.S. Kresge. Austin made his stake by discovering a gas pocket under Pittston and selling it to the city then officially a borough. He described his business on his letterhead "Hardware, Tinning, and Plumbing." In the 1890's, the coal collieries were among his best clients. They needed furnaces to heat the breakers in winter and fans to vent the shafts into the mine workings. Pat McNulty's Saloon, a crowded lively place, inhabited the area of 24 South Main Street. Mr. C.A. Stroh's Drugstore was busy serving customers at 30 South Main Street.

As the horses and buggies passed by, the dust circulated from their hoofs. The men and women were dressed in different clothes depending on their wealth and class. Male shop keepers were outside their stores with brooms and pails of water trying to keep their windows clean. They greeted the people on their side-walk who may be potential customers in the future. As the new immigrants walked by, the townspeople looked at them with surprise and dismay because the immigrants' clothes and shoes were not what the townspeople expected. Because of two weeks of travel by boat, the immigrants' clothes were dirty. People in the apartments above were looking down at the new immigrant arrivals. Because of the language barrier, the people would smile, nod their head, or wave.

A large building located between 31-37 South Main Street housed Freed Jewelers, Clarke Brothers Department Store, and Anthony Forlenza's Con-fection Store. Mr. Forlenza was one of the first Italian immigrants in Pittston.

As Rocco, Maria, Carlo, and Victoria walked by, he greeted them with a big hug. He always welcomed the Italian immigrants and told them he would help them with any of their needs. He gave Maria and Rocco a small package of candy as a welcoming gift. He held Michael in his arms and kissed him on his cheek. As one of the first Italians in Pittston, he was proud of his heritage and welcomed everyone to his home.

The Odd Fellows Hall opened at 57 South Main Street. They came into being as a counter to the Masons. To join the Masons, which can be traced back to guilds of stonemasons in Europe in the 15th century, one had to be a mason. The Odd Fellows were formed in England in the 18ᵗʰ century as a fraternity for men of the odd trades, such as laborers and miners. The Odd Fellows Thistle Lodge was founded in Pittston in 1852. The Thistle Lodge, a miners' lodge, served its members in time of injury, illness, and death, keeping families together. In the past, the Odd Fellows were known for founding and taking care of cemeteries. The Odd Fellows founded the Pittston Cemetery in 1857 and passed it on to the Pittston Cemetery Association in 1884.

Phillip Bianco owned a shoemaker shop at 63 South Main Street, and the site of Paul Bohan's General Store was 67-69 Main Street. There was always a large crowd at Perna's Café and Bowling Academy located at 71 South Main Street. It was a popular place, and many people liked to bowl.

Carlo and Victoria and Maria and Rocco holding babies, Michael and Rosa crossed the street at the Knights of Columbus located at 77 South Main Street. On the corner of Market Street and South Main streets was a hardware building. On the top floor of 78 North Main Street, Carlo and Victoria rented their apartment. It was a three-room apartment with sparse furnishings. There was a coal stove, and Victoria immediately put a pot of water on the stove for Rocco and Maria to wash in a wooden tub located in the back room. When the water was warm, they washed Michael and Rosa first and then Maria took off her clothes to get into the tub. It was such a relief to take a bath after two weeks on the boat. Rocco helped Maria get from the tub and then he washed. Victoria cooked a delicious dinner for their first evening in America with anise cookies for dessert. After dinner Carlo went to work the nightshift in the coal mine. Victoria was watching children for a wealthy family on William Street.

As it started to get dark, there were twenty-six arc lights and 168 incandescent street lights furnished by the Citizens' Electric Illuminating Company, which automatically came on after dark. It seemed as if people were always on the main street throughout the night.

After Maria took the ribbon from her hair, she brushed her hair for a while. Rocco watched as his beautiful wife undressed for bed. It was their first night in America and it was their first time alone together. This was a night they would always remember. They were in love, and the thought of being alone was very exciting. Their new life was beginning, and they looked forward to their future in America.

*Chapter 6*

## MAIN STREET- SUNDAY MORNING

Maria and Rocco awoke early the next morning to the ringing of the church bells. It was Sunday, a day of rest and time to be with their families. They prepared breakfast and everyone dressed in their best clothes to attend church services. Victoria made Maria's skirt and blouse to wear on Sunday. Rocco dressed in the clothes he brought from Italy. As they walked up the sidewalk with babies Michael and Rosa in their arms, they were met by throngs of people going in all directions to attend their church. Families with small children nestled close to their bodies and older children walking alongside their parents filled the sidewalk. All of the stores and businesses, including the coal mines, were closed on Sunday. It was a day to give thanks for all their blessings and for their safe journey to America. Some people rode in carriages and dressed in fine colorful clothing. Others were dressed in very conservative outfits. All the men wore hats, and the women had a scarf, veil, or shawl covering their head.

There were many different nationalities in Pittston and each had their own church. At this time, there wasn't an urgency to learn English because people stayed and socialized with their fellow countrymen. At this time, there wasn't an Italian church, and Italians were welcome to worship in any church. Some would walk the distance to north Pittston to attend Mass at Saint Mary's, the first Catholic church erected.

At the beginning of the nineteenth century, a number of Irish families attracted to this promising valley by the opening of the anthracite coal fields brought with them the religious spirit for which the Irish have long been noted.

During the years of 1837 to 1849, the homes of Thomas McCue and Michael Reap and the Daley family became the stopping place for missionary priests until the building of the first church in 1851.

Reverend Henry Fitzsimmons, stationed in Carbondale, was the first priest to make regular visits to the Catholics of Pittston and the surrounding area. In 1846 Reverend Patrick Pendergast succeeded Father Fitzsimmons.

In 1849 Reverend Basil Shorb, who succeeded Father Pendergast, secured the piece of land on the hill-known afterwards as Church Hill, then Chapel Street, and encouraged the building of the first church. Father Shorb was succeeded by Reverend John Loughran.

In the summer of 1851, the dream was realized when the first Catholic church in the North Wyoming Valley was blessed. For the first time, in a building specially dedicated to the service of God, Holy Mass was offered. Some of the founding members were Thomas McCue and Michael Reap.

Old Saint Mary's was not securely erected. No pews were installed, but families disposed to do so placed moveable benches in the church. The members of this scattered parish, which constituted the entire Pittston Area and surrounding towns, were required to attend Saint Mary's.

In 1881 the Catholic families of Upper Pittston desired the construction of another building of their own to replace the first church erected in 1851. This was accomplished under the direction of Father John J. Finnen. The second Saint Mary's occupied the same spot, as did the First Saint Mary's. Built in 1882, it was blessed by the Most Reverend William O'Hara,D.D., Bishop of Scranton, on May 6th, 1883. This was a substantial frame building with basement and gallery. The church served the faithful of Upper Pittston for years until the construction in 1905 of the third Saint Mary, Help of Christians Church, at its present site on North Main Street.

As Rocco, Maria, and the children walked to attend church, they passed T. A. Grace at 72 South Main Street. A large sign in the window read, "When buying groceries, remember that comparison is the only test of value. Prices alone make no article cheap. Quality is equally necessary. We believe our goods represent quality." They were in the Welsh Building, which also housed A. J. Frushon Fruits.

Evans Brothers Shoes and Groceries opened their store at 44-46 South Main Street. In the newspaper, they advertised the lowest prices with high quality goods.

Week's Brothers had their store at 14 South Main Street. As Maria and Rocco reached the corner of Main and Broad Streets, they were amazed by the four-story Miners' Savings Bank building, a tan and grey building with large windows. Many businesses and merchants had their offices and stores on the upper floors.

They could see many women dressed in dark dresses and hats going into The First Presbyterian Church on Broad Street. It is a long, grey rectangular church with a high steeple. As Maria and Rocco crossed the street near them, the women were very cordial and welcoming with smiles and waves. The Presbyterian Church traces its ancestry primarily to England and Scotland. The church members generally exhibit their faith through acts of generosity, hospitality, and the constant pursuit of social justice, as well as proclamation of the gospel of Christ.

The seeds of the First Presbyterian Church were sown February 25th, 1842 when the Presbyterian Church of Lackawanna was founded in what was called "the Atherton Neighborhood," now the Borough of Taylor. This church served all Presbyterians from Pittston Township, Pittston City, and all outlying boroughs east of the Susquehanna River. The Pittston City section of the township was then called Pittston Ferry.

Later in 1842, Theodore Strong started a Presbyterian Sunday School in a small red schoolhouse in Upper Pittston. Shortly thereafter services were held in the same building. Services were conducted in private homes near the schoolhouse. The people who spurred this movement included: Theodore Strong, William Atherton, Elder Elijah Coucham, Elder John M. Atherton, and First Deacon Thomas Bailey.

In 1844 Nathan Grier Parke was authorized to preach and conduct prayer meetings in Pittston as a stop on horseback circuit ministry. On July 7th, 1846, he was ordained as a Presbyterian minister and continued to serve the Pittston church until 1895, a period of fifty years.

In 1874 the Melanie Chapel was built in North Pittston, directly behind the 1846 Presbyterian church. The chapel was named in honor of Dr. and Mrs. Parke's daughter, Melanie, for her work with children. In 1936 the deserted chapel was deemed a fire hazard and torn down. Currently the Melanie Cemetery can be found on the left side of north Main Street. The English, Scotch, and Welsh were major groups in Pittston. They immigrated to America in the early 1800's and held major offices in local government and were proprietors of many businesses.

As Maria and Rocco and the children, along with Carlo and Victoria, came to the corner, there was a long row of stores located at 1-3-5-7 North Main Street. This was called the Cash Store Block. These stores were cash-only sales. There were many items in the windows showing the prices of the goods. Barry the Jeweler and the 5 Cent Store were located close to this area.

On the corner of North Main and William Streets was the First National Bank of Pittston also known as the Pittston Bank. The oldest bank in Pittston was first located at the west side of North Main Street on the site occupied by the Boston Shoe Store. As they turned the corner, the Masonic Lodge was built at 1 William Street. The steeples of Saint John the Evangelist church could be seen from a distance, and now they were walking beneath them.

Reverend John P. O'Shaughnessy became the first resident Catholic pastor in Pittston. Having secured a lot on William Street in October 1853, Father O'Shaughnessy set about erecting the first church of Saint John the Evangelist. The church that was built was a small, wooden, rectangular building erected on the site of the present church, corner of William and Church Street, Pittston.

On September 20th, 1858, Reverend John Finnen was appointed by Bishop Neumann to assist Father O'Shaughnessy. Father O'Shaughnessy died on February 17th, 1862. In May of 1859, Reverend Patrick Prendergast was transferred to Pittston to succeed Father O'Shaughnessy. He labored assiduously in the mission for two and a half years. He died in the pastoral home on November 2nd, 1861.

Upon Father Prendergast's death, Father Finnen was immediately placed in charge of Saint John the Evangelist Church. Under his direction, the Catholics of Pittston made a number of far reaching improvements. In 1863 Father Finnen purchased a double brick dwelling next to the church for a school and residence of the Sisters who would have charge of instruction. The nuns placed in charge were from the Order of the Immaculate Heart of Mary of Reading, Pennsylvania.

The Diocese of Philadelphia, of which Pittston was part, divided in 1868, and on March 3rd of that year, the new Diocese of Scranton was established. On the July 12th, 1868, Reverend William O'Hara was consecrated the first Bishop of Scranton.

In the winter of 1887, it was decided the first church was too small and a new one should be built. The old church was demolished, and Masses were held in the school building.

During the Christmas holidays of 1887 and 1888, a great fair (The Christmas Argosy) was held in Keystone Hall at the corner of South Main and Pine streets. The object of the fair was to begin a fund for the erection of a new Roman Catholic church building. The architect chosen was Edwin Forest Durang of Philadelphia and the contractor was Edward Delaney of the same city. He also built Saint John's Convent next to the church.

The cornerstone of the new Saint John the Evangelist Church was laid September 22nd, 1889. This cornerstone also showed the date of 1854, from the other wooden church, on the William Street side. The estimated cost of the new church was $150,000. This four-year project resulted in a beautiful Gothic edifice considered a landmark in Luzerne County.

The ceremony of the dedication was held on April 16th, 1893. At the conclusion of the Mass, Reverend Bishop O'Hara spoke briefly to the congregation. He congratulated the people on laboring faithfully and unitedly for the accomplishment of this grand church. "It is the jewel of the Diocese." Aided by preconstruction fund raising by the parishioners, most either Irish immigrants or their offspring, the parish was debt-free when the church was formally dedicated.

At the age of seventy-one, Father Finnen died at the residence on February 14th, 1899. He served the longest tenure of any pastor, having served from 1861 to 1899.

The next pastor assigned was Reverend Eugene A. Garvey. In March 1900, he was one of the incorporators of Saint John High School, along with Bishop Michael Hoban, Paul Bohan, Sister M. Conception, and M.W. Morris. Father Garvey was selected to lead the Diocese in Altoona.

Replacing Father Garvey was Reverend John P. O'Malley. He came to Saint John the Evangelist with great zeal and earnestness. Later he became a monsignor, and during his tenure, the parish celebrated its fiftieth anniversary.

As Maria and Rocco and the children entered the church, they could hear the choir singing. They were amazed at this beautiful structure, which was built of Trenton stone and trimmed with light Indiana limestone. The completed building, which measures 160 feet by 62 feet, has artistically superb stained-glass windows throughout.

The towering twin spires were topped with gilded crosses add to the overall beauty of the structure, attracting attention from throughout the Pittston community, both on the east and west sides of the Susquehanna River.

The entire structure was made of stone and wood with the exception of the metal posts holding up the balcony and the main floor. The beams were installed in a way to support the roof without pillars.

Maria and Rocco were in awe of the main altar built of white marble. The two side altars were also constructed of marble, as was the sanctuary and altar rail. The nave was designed to seat 1,500 people, while the gallery holds 400.

As Maria and Rocco with Rosa and Michael in his arms, and Carlo and Victoria took their seats in the back, they listened to the beautiful organ music and the choir singing. Worshippers filled all seats on the main floor and the gallery. There were pews reserved in front, on the left, for certain parishioners. Later Maria and Rocco learned that the coal mine owners, mine bosses, and engineers sat there. Father O'Malley offered the Mass, and although Rocco and Maria didn't understand English, they felt welcome by his demeanor and glance. Most of the parishioners at Saint John the Evangelist Church had light complexions, blue eyes, and blond or red hair. They immigrated from Ireland because of the Irish Potato Famine of 1845 to 1852 when the potato crop failed in successive years. The crop failures were caused by late blight, a disease that destroys both the leaves and edible tubers of the potato plant. This period of mass starvation in Ireland was the main reason Irish immigrants came to America.

By 1870 more than 4,000 native Irish lived in Pittston. This was over half the city's total population of 7,500. In some areas, there was resistance of the Irish influx and some of the industry's infamous "No Irish Need Apply" signs were posted in the Pittston area. Soon, however, the anthracite industry demand for labor was high, and the Irish immigrants found work in the mines and ancillary industries and started businesses.

The Friendly Sons of Saint Patrick was founded in 1913. Their mission statement was to pay tribute to the Patron Saint of Ireland by fostering good will and fellowship among those of Irish ancestry and the Greater Pittston community through social, cultural, and charitable events.

As Maria, Rocco, and the others were leaving to go home for Sunday dinner, parishioners exited Saint John the Baptist church across the street. In early 1890's, the people of Slovak descent came from Slovakia (then Austria-Hungary). Many of them settled in the anthracite regions of Luzerne and Lackawanna counties. These immigrants were endowed not only with physical stamina, which enabled them to find work in the coal mines, but also with a spiritual fervor and zeal, which prompted them to continue their religious practices and customs which they felt would be best achieved by organizing their own parish.

In 1892 Slovaks living within a radius of ten miles, purchased a church building located on William Street in Pittston for $5,000. It was owned by German Catholics who decided to build a new church on top of the hill on Church Street. This German church was in close proximity of William Street. Bishop William O'Hara appointed Father Albert Kazincy, the first Slovak priest ordained for service in the Diocese of Scranton, to be the first pastor of Saint John the Baptist Church.

Because the parish was growing at such a fast rate, the second pastor, Father Matthew Jankola, began plans for a new church, which was dedicated in 1902, replacing the old wooden structure. Father Andrew Pavco, the third pastor, built the rectory in 1915 and the school in 1917. The Congregation of the Sisters of Saints Cyril and Methodius served the school as teachers.

The longest tenure as pastor was held by Monsignor Joseph J. Super, who served as an assistant pastor, then pastor. For over forty years, Monsignor Super dedicated his ministry not only to the people of the parish community but to the students who attended Saint John the Baptist Elementary School.

Maria and Rocco and Carlo and Victoria went to Frank's apartment for Sunday dinner. Frank started the dinner with a wine toast to Maria and Rocco and their children. He was happy they arrived safely and would start their new life's journey in America. Frank gave clothes and boots to Rocco to wear in the coal mines. After eating soup and homemade apple pie, Rocco and Maria walked back to Carlo and Victoria's apartment on South Main Street. After Maria nursed the children, they fell to sleep quickly. They needed to go to sleep early because Rocco had to apply for a job at the Pennsylvania Coal Company. Rocco and Maria made passionate love and fell asleep in each other's arms. Soon Maria was pregnant, and they welcomed their third child Dominick.

# Chapter 7

## THE COAL MINING INDUSTRY

The next morning, Rocco kissed Maria and the children goodbye and went with Carlo Romano, his father-in-law, to apply for a job at the Pennsylvania Coal Company. The Pennsylvania Coal Company office was located on Wharf Street, and its alternate name was the Erie Coal Company because it was owned by the Erie Railroad. When Carlo and Rocco arrived, there was a long line of men waiting to apply for work. As he approached the office, Rocco was met by a person taking names. Everyone was assigned a number that was written on a piece of paper and handed to them. Rocco was very nervous with the thought that he may not be accepted for work in the coal mines. There were men from different countries applying for jobs. Many languages were being spoken at the same time, which confused Rocco. There were company men available to translate in all languages. The paper presented to apply for the laborer position was very brief with just a few questions, such as the applicants name, address, and the name of a person to contact if the workers were injured. A company doctor gave physicals to determine if the men were able-bodied enough to work in the coal mine. The doctor's main objective was to observe the posture and body build, which was important for working as a laborer. Those who limped or had bad posture were not allowed to work in the coal mine. Many were given jobs inside the breaker, but others were turned away. Most secured a job as laborers because the main requirement was to load the coal into the cars. The pay rate was sixty-three cents an hour.

Rocco was accepted for the laborer position. He was told to report for work at No. 6, the Pennsylvania Coal Company in Jenkins Township, Pennsylvania. The next morning, his brother-in-law, Frank Romano, walked with him to the mine. Frank was also employed at the coal mine. Many men walked in the same direction because there were a few collieries in that area. The No. 6 Colliery of the Pennsylvania Coal Company was a massive structure built in 1898. It stood seven stories high with many different levels and hundreds of windows. Many smaller outer buildings needed for various uses in the coal industry lined the area. The men waited in line for instructions to be provided by another mine worker assigned to the newly hired laborers. The word "mine worker" applied to all employees in or around a colliery, regardless of occupation. They included subterranean men and boys, such as miners, subcontractors, laborers, haulers, fire bosses, mine foreman, nippers (boy door tenders), driver boys (young mule drivers), and stablemen (mule tenders).

FIGURE 9. NO.6 COLLIERY, PENNSYLVANIA COAL COMPANY, JENKINS TWP. PA. BUILT 1898, NATIONAL CANAL MUSEUM ARCHIVES.

Although the men working in the mine came from different countries, they all had a common goal, to make a living wage, enabling them and their families to survive in America. Two hours before the men entered the mine, the fires bosses tested for poisonous methane gas, which could explode within in the mine and cause injury or death to the mine workers. After they assessed that the area was safe for work, they would put their initials and date on the wall of coal.

The men were separated into three-man teams with two laborers assigned to work with a miner. Some of the miners would start as breaker boys, picking slate in the breaker at age ten or twelve and then they went underground as a driver boy. As they got older, they worked their way up to a laborer and then worked toward getting their Anthracite Miners' Certificate. Some older men started out as laborers, and after working many years, were able to qualify to be a miner.

Rocco and another laborer followed the miner to the cage, which would be lowered into the mine with the empty wooden coal car. As they descended into the ground for the first time and could not see the outside brightness of day, there was a feeling in Rocco's stomach that he would never forget for the rest of his life. It was unnerving to go below the ground to work and it was something he hoped his children would never have to experience. It took time to reach the area they were assigned to work and to get used to breathing in this atmosphere. They rolled the mine car onto the track to get to the area ready to be worked. The miner was well-aware of their concerns and tried to make them feel comfortable. It was very dark with only the light from their open-flame, oil wick lamps. The miner uses a hand auger to drill holes for placing powder charges to blast out the coal. The holes were then packed with a squib charge of black powder, covered with dirt, fused, and set off. After the blast, there would be plenty of large chunks of coal to load into the empty coal car. There was always a danger of the roof caving in and seriously injuring or killing the coal miners. This particular area had timbers bracing the roof. The laborers loaded two large coal cars filled with coal. The coal had to be above the rim of the coal car. It was hard, tedious work but work that had to be done to remove the anthracite coal from the earth. At that point, the miner went to signal to the mule driver that two cars were ready to be removed from the mine.

The mule driver and mules were very important to the mining operation. The driver and the mule were together for eight to ten hours a day. After work the driver put the mule in the stable, took off his harness, and cleaned the area. He was required to feed and groom the mule. In the morning, the driver would be one of the first in the mine. He would go to the stable to get the mule hitched up and ready to pull the empty cars into the mine.

When the mule driver came with the mule to pull the cars to the foot of the mine shaft to be hoisted to the surface, Rocco was stunned to see the mule driver was a very frail, young man of about fourteen-years-old. He had a well-worn handmade, cut-plait whip around his neck. He wore high boots because of all the water that was in the mine. His cap had an emblem on the top. His job was very dangerous with the possibility of being kicked by the stubborn mules or squeezed into the mine wall. The mule would pull the loaded coal cars to the foot of the mine shaft where they would be hoisted to the surface, and once on the surface, the mules would move the coal cars to the breaker. The mules were very smart and stubborn.

The miner put the number assigned to the laborers on the coal cars and the weighmen would weigh each car to make sure credit was given to the laborers for their work.

At the end of the day, Rocco talked to some of his fellow Italians who also started to work that morning. They noticed children dressed with the same coats and hats coming from the breaker. After eating lunch, the children started to play ball. Rocco couldn't imagine why children were at the coal breaker. Hours later, at the end of the day, Rocco walked over to the coal breaker. He could see the coal cars going up the side of the breaker and the coal being dumped into the breaker. The function of the breaker was to break coal into pieces and sort these pieces into categories of nearly uniform size; this process is known as breaking. Fuel for the early American Industrial Revolution, anthracite coal, underwent little processing before being sent to market, which was primarily for iron works. Use of the breaker boys began around 1860. They worked ten-hour days, six days a week on wooden seats perched over the conveyor belts, picking slate and other impurities out of the coal. Breaker Boys were forced to work without gloves, so that they could better handle the slick coal. The slate was sharp, and the Breaker Boys would often leave work with their fingers cut and bleeding. Some had their fingers, arms, or legs cut off. Many were crushed to death, and their bodies weren't recovered until the end of the shift. There were approximately 13,000 Breaker Boys working in 1902 and as high as 24,000 by 1907.

FIGURE 10. BREAKER BOYS (LIBRARY OF CONGRESS, LEWIS HINE COLLECTION)

As Rocco walked into the breaker, he could see the children sitting in rows picking out the slate and rock from the coal that was coming down between their legs. Everything was black from the coal dust, and the children were inhaling this dust. A foreman was walking around the children with a whip in his hand. Rocco would always remember this disturbing site. As he walked home with Frank, it was the topic of their conversation. These little "Breaker Boys" were the bravest children in the world. They needed to work to help their families survive. Their fathers worked in the coal mine while they were working in the breaker. At this time, there were no child labor laws and children did not have to attend school.

FIGURE 11. BREAKER BOYS (LIBRARY OF CONGRESS, LEWIS HINE COLLECTION)

When Rocco reached the apartment, Maria was waiting for him with soup and homemade bread. Rocco, covered with black dust in the mine, took a bath in the wooden tub in the back room of the apartment. Maria asked him about his first day of working in the coal mine. He told her about the work and going below ground for the first time. He didn't tell Maria about the dangers of this work. Also, he never told Maria about the children working in the breaker. After dinner he held Dominick in his arms until his little boy fell asleep.

As he was lying next to Maria, he kept thinking about the day. It was a long journey to America, and he wanted to make it worthwhile for his family. It was noisy outside on South Main Street. There were many taverns and saloons to accommodate the miners and others coming from work.

Many thought it was a good idea to have a shot of whiskey and a beer to clear their throat of the mine dust.

After working hard all week at the coal mine, it was finally Sunday and time to go to church and spend time with their family. As Carlo and Victoria prepared breakfast, Maria and Rocco got dressed to go to church. They decided to go the far end of North Main Street to visit the Saint Mary's Church on the hill in Pittston Junction. Soon this old wooden church would be closing and the new brick church would open on North Main Street.

## List of Coal Breakers in the Greater Pittston Area Courtesy of Richard Fitzsimmons Ph.D.

- The Ravine Breaker, North Main Street, Pittston owned by Mr. Hines and later the Kehoe-Berge Coal Company.
- Old Seneca Breaker, Lambert Street, Pittston, owned by Cowan and Dinniny.
- Seneca Breaker, 2, Located south of Twin breaker owned by Newton Coal Company and later by Kehoe-Berge Coal Company.
- Cork and Bottle Braker, Cork Lane Section, Pittston Township along the Delaware and Hudson Railroad tracks.
- Breaker of the Pennsylvania Coal Company #6.
- The Mount Lookout Breaker, Wyoming Avenue, Exeter.
- The Exeter Breaker of the Lehigh Valley Coal Company, later owned by Kehoe-Berge Coal Company.
- The Joe Cake Breaker
- The Sullivan Trail Breaker of the Pagnotti Coal Company, also owned by independent operators Joe Cake, Archy Dewitt.
- The Stevens Breaker, Pittston Junction, owned by the Newton Coal Company and later Kehoe- Berge Coal Company.
- The Twin Breaker, Pittston Junction, owner Newton Coal Company and later Kehoe-Berge Coal Company.
- The old #10 Breaker on Parsonage Street operated by Pa. Coal Co.
- The old #8 Breaker in (Hamtown)(former name of Hughestown) Pa. Coal Co.
- The Paradise Breaker, owned by Cowen and Dininny, located between Hughestown and West Avoca, operated by S.P. Bennett.
- The Old Breaker of Boston Settlement, first operated by Cowen and Dininny, and later by Pasquale Adonizio, better known as "Tony Rose".
- The Old Heidelberg Breaker owned by Lehigh Valley Coal Company and operated by Pa. Coal Co., which was in Pittston Township. It was

located just a few hundred yards beyond the Butler Breaker along the state highway.

- Heidelberg Breaker operated by John B. McDade, of Scranton, which is in Dupont Borough, which at one time was part of Pittston.
- The Butler Breaker, which is between Pittston and Dupont operated by Pa. Coal Co.
- The Florence Breaker in Dupont.
- The Hillside Breaker , Avoca, originally owned by the Hillside Coal and Iron Company and later sold to Pa.Coal Co. and later sold to Tommy Quinn, Scranton.
- The Langcliff Breaker, Avoca, operated by individuals.
- The Drybred Breaker, Avoca, operated by C.C. Bowman and W.H. Hollister.
- The Central Breaker, Avoca, operated by Pa. Coal Co.
- The Phoenix Breaker the viaduct in Duryea, owned by D.L.&W Coal Company.
- The Big Push, or Hurry Up, Breaker, Duryea.Owned by Mears and Flynn and later the Kehoe-Berge Coal Company.
- The Hallstead, or Red Ball Breaker, operated by individuals, later by the Glen Alden Coal Colmpany. Later, the Kehoe-Berge Coal Company.
- The Dying Dog Breaker, Duryea, operated by the Simpson & Watkins. It was as called the Pig and Whistle Breaker. Owned by Tommy Watkins and the Simpson Family.
- The Sturnersville Breaker, Exeter, owned by Cowen and Dininny, when Exeter was known as Sturnersville.
- The Muddy Creek (Brook) Breaker, Exeter, operated by Cowen and Dininny.
- The # 14 Breaker, Port Blanchard Section, operated by Charles Gelso.
- The Lawrence Breaker, Old Forge, owned by Robinson and Law.
- The Katy Did Breaker, along Spring Brook Road, Moosic, owned by Robinson and Law.
- The Muskrat Breaker, along the Moosic-Daleville Highway.
- The Hannas Breaker, owned by the Lehigh Valley Coal Company.
- The Last Chance Breaker, operated by the Kehoe-Berge Coal Company.

- # 9 Breaker, Hughestown, operated by the Pagnotti Coal Company.
- The Old Forge Breaker, which adjoins Duryea Borough.
- The Shimmy Breaker, Avoca, along the Delaware, Lackawanna and Western Railroad.
- The William A.Breaker, later abandoned, but the Kehoe-Berge Breaker was build, circa 1933, at approximately the same location, as the most modern breaker in the world.
- The Simpson-Watkins Breaker- The Kehoe-Berge Coal Company.
- The #9 Breaker, Hughestown, operated by the Pagnotti Coal Company.
- The Kehoe-Berge Coal Company Breaker, Duryea,circa 1933.
- The Ewen Breaker, Port Griffith, operated by the PA. Coal Company.

# Chapter 8

## A Trolley Ride Along South Main Street
## and North Main Street

Rocco, Maria, Rosa, and Michael boarded the trolley, The Scranton and Pittston Traction Company opened a trolley line on June 27th, 1896. The Moosic/Pittston trolley line entered Luzerne County at the north end of Avoca and followed Main Street through Avoca and entered Dupont. At the south end of Dupont, the line again left the highway and turned west, crossing the Lehigh Valley Railroad mountain cut-off and the Delaware and Hudson Railroad on a long steel viaduct, then the line turned south along the public road through Hughestown and into Pittston, turning onto William Street, then onto Fulton Street, where it went south to Broad and to North Main Street.

Trolley travel was a new experience for Rocco and Maria because there were no trolleys in southern Italy. The very kind, courteous conductor smiled as everyone boarded at the corner of Broad and North Main Streets. People of different nationalities boarded and Rocco and Maria shared their row with other city residents. Even though they didn't understand English, a kind wave or smile was enough to let fellow passengers know they were welcome. As they traveled slowly up North Main Street, they were able to see the interesting well-kept stores on North Main Street.

FIGURE 12. TROLLEY ON MAIN STREET (COURTESY JULIO CAPRARI)

B.F. Antrim and Company at 3 North Main Street was the oldest dry good store in Pittston. They advertised they had the largest inventory of goods in Pittston. Located at 5 North Main Street was George F. Buss tailor and above his store was Gilroy Real Estate. The Globe Dry Goods was at 9 North Main Street and Dr. Charles J. McFadden had his office on the second floor. Markus and Brothers clothiers were located at 11 North Main Street. At 13 North Main, William Drury had a grocery store. Bernard Oppenheimer operated a men's store at 31 North Main Street. Brown and Company Groceries sold their goods at 33 North Main Street.

L&F Seibel Meat Market opened at 35 North Main Street had many different meats hanging in its window. At this time, the trolley stopped and passengers left the trolley and others boarded. Mr. Abraham Yelen was outside his store at 41 North Main Street washing down the windows and awnings. Cohen Brothers clothing store owned by Sam and Morris Cohen opened at 55 North Main Street. Merchant tailors, Marcus and Feldman, were next door at 57 North Main Street. A large store at 65-67 North Main Street was the location of Sacks and Brown.

Butler House, a large boarding house for new immigrants and visitors passing through opened at 71 North Main Street. This four-story building dated back to the Reconstruction period following the Civil War and served as a hotel for a city bustling with travelers and immigrants. It featured solid oak walls and floors.

Sinclair House was another boarding house at the corner of Butler and North Main Streets. Many lodgers would stay only one night. Men and women could be seen leaving at all hours of the morning.

W.C. Price drugs-medicines-chemicals operated one of the first drug stores near the Armory Block where the Armory Clothing Store and B.F. Cooper Furniture were situated at 91 North Main Street. At 93 North Main Street was a firearms and ammunition store. At this point, all of the passengers got off the trolley and continued to walk to the church.

Nearing the Pittston Ferry Bridge, they saw the Toll Office at 119 North Main Street. Opposite the Ferry Bridge on the corner of Mill Street was the Chicago Cash Store. Kizis's Saloon occupied the site of 179 North Main Street.

The" Kashuba Hotel" opened at 197 Main Street. Peter Paul Kashuba was born on June 27th, 1859 in Lithuania, then a part of Russia. He immigrated to the United States from Bremen and Germany, arriving in New York on June 1st, 1878 with his brother Mathias and wife Maria. In 1880 he married Hannah (Anna) Schevits, who was born in Austria in April 1858.

James A. Joyce opened a meat and general merchandise store at 209-213 North Main Street.

A few blocks away was Church Hill, now called Chapel Street, where Saint Mary's, the small first Roman Catholic Church, was built on the top of the hill.

As the church bells rang, Maria and Rocco climbed the hill to enter the church. This church, built in the same spot as the first Saint Mary's church, was larger and had a basement. Twenty wooden pews lined each side. Maria, Rocco, and the children took a seat. Beautiful white lace covered the simple wooden altar. A large wooden cross, with the image of Jesus, was in the middle of the church wall behind the altar. The priest offered Mass, and everyone received Communion. People sang beautiful hymns from the books provided in the pews. As they left the church, they could hear the organ playing.

*FIGURE 13. JAMES RYAN STONEWARE (PHOTO BY MARY T. POLICARE)*

North of Church Hill was James Ryan Stoneware built at 464 North Main Street. A large general store at 550-552 North Main Street was owned by Thomas Maloney and Michael Reap, two well-known Pittston residents. Nearby was the Saint James Hotel.

The Home Market was at 120 North Main Street. Morris Yaseen Confection had his store at 116 N. Main Street. Frank A. Patience had an upholstery and cabinet store at 108 North Main Street. C. C. Garrison sold hand guns and rifles at 104 North Main Street.

As Maria and Rocco looked to the left, they could see the top of the Saint John's Evangelical Lutheran Church on Wood Street. This large, red brick church was established on November 22$^{nd}$, 1857. When the church was first founded, it was referred to as a German church. Everything was written and spoken in German. In May 1858, Saint John's was granted acceptance to the Pennsylvania Ministerium, which was the first North American Lutheran Church body. In the early years of St. John's, services were in German. English services began in 1895. In 1917 a new church was built on the site of the old church, which was braced, put on rollers, and moved out of the way. Church members supplied the labor for the move.

Soon they passed Parsonage Street where the Second Presbyterian Church had its beginning in 1893. Although many of the Italian immigrants coming into Pittston near the turn of the century were Catholics, there were a few Protestants among them. Reverend Vitale became the first ordained minister to the Italian mission. In 1908 a new chapel was erected on Parsonage Street, and in 1912, improvements were made at the church. The erection of the chapel established the fact of a permanent Italian Protestant Church in the City of Pittston.

The Tavern was owned by John C. Kehoe and his brother Thomas Kehoe and was opened at 62 North Main Street.

The Eagle Hotel, built at 46 North Main Street, was a large wooden four-story building. This hotel catered to many businessmen, immigrants, and residents of Pittston. The second floor had a large wrap around porch for everyone staying at the hotel. There were three street entrances and four display windows located in front of the hotel. A large restaurant the length of the building was on the left side. On the lower level, there was a barber shop and clothes cleaners. There was a livery stable in the back. Brown and Company, owned by Walter Cohen, was one of the earliest stores located at 38 North Main Street. Louis Schiffman had a shoe store at 34 North Main Street. When Mr. Schiffman retired, his son Joseph Schiffman became owner of the Boston Shoe Store.

At the same time that the Jewish immigrants flocked to Wilkes-Barre's Heights, they came in smaller numbers to nearly every town of any size in Luzerne County. Often joining relatives in a particular town, they lived in communities on both sides of the Susquehanna River, from Duryea and Avoca and Scranton, north of Wilkes-Barre, to Shickshinny and Mocanaqua, south of Wilkes-Barre.

Anthracite coal mining was central to the economies of most of the towns, and the Jewish immigrants, soon opened shops that served the miners. Storekeepers and their large families usually lived above or behind their Main street stores, where their children also worked when they weren't tending younger siblings or attending school.

In Pittston the first Jewish immigrants established a beneficial society to aid members in time of sickness. According to the charter recorded January 26th, 1875, officers of Ahaovs Achim Society of Brotherly Love were Adolph Fleischer, Simon Feldman, Levi Goodman, and Abraham Allgaier, while Henry Cohen, Gabriel David, and Simon Mendel served as trustees. Pittston's first East European Jews, Abraham Roginsky and Joseph Freed and their families, arrived in 1881 and soon formed the nucleus of a traditional congregation. They began to meet for religious services in 1887, first at Freed's home, then at Jacob Shoestein's home By then, thirty Jewish families lived in Pittston.

The first of these was Jewish Congregation Agudas Achim of Pittston, which applied for a charter on November 25th, 1903. Subscribers to the charter were Joseph Goldberg, Joseph Moskewitz, Harry W. Yoseen, J. Freed, David Feldman, Jacob Shoestein, Farkas Engel, M. Yoseen, J. Baroff, M. Lichterman, Charles Wolf, H. Cooplan, Louis Schiffman, and Abe Roginsky.

With Jacob Shoestein as first president, the congregation decided to move services to the Butler Building on North Main Street. Later the congregation used the Odd Fellows and Knights of Columbus buildings on South Main Street for services.

Coursen Hardware Co house furnishings sold its goods at 30 North Main Street. Corcoran Brothers advertised the finest hats, scarves, and gloves at 28 North Main Street. Joel Brenton, a painter, had a paint store at 24 North Main. Isadore Gompertz department store opened at 20 Main Street. Walter Barritt's Paint Store was also in this block. A very young boy named Anthony Bantell worked in the store and learned the paint business. Later he opened Bantell's Paint store at this site.

The Pittston Gazette was started by G. M. Richart and H. S. Phillips on August 2nd, 1850. The first home of the Pittston Gazette was the Long Store Building at 73 S. Main Street. Mr. William Peck became owner and publisher of the Pittston Gazette on May 7th, 1901. Tallie Evans was editor all of the years Mr. Peck owned the Pittston Gazette. Later the Pittston Gazette newspaper opened at 16 North Main Street.

R. B. Cutler Furniture and Undertaking had a duel business at 14 North Main Street. McAndrew Brothers Pool Room located at 12 North Main Street had a crowd of men waiting to go into their establishment. C.R. Andrews books and envelopes opened at 10 North Main Street.

Rocco, Maria, and the children came to the corner of Willliam and North Main Street. They could see the Howell and King Brewery on the corner of Cron Street. The brewery was erected in 1860. Anthony Forlenza waved to them from the entrance of his confectionery shop. He practiced in the rear of his store with his fellow musicians. They were all members of the Columbian Italian Band. He was a member of the committee, which helped organize Our Lady of Mount Carmel Church

Congregation and assisted in the purchase of the initial church property at 131 William Street. He was excited to let Rocco and Maria know that the paperwork was complete and the first Italian Catholic Church, in Pittston, would soon become a reality.

When they arrived at Victoria and Carlo's apartment, Maria was very tired and didn't feel well. In nine months, they welcomed their fourth child Victoria. Victoria was an adorable happy baby with light brown hair.

# Chapter 9

## OUR LADY OF MOUNT CARMEL CHURCH
## AND A VISIT FROM PRESIDENT THEODORE ROOSEVELT

In the summer of 1904, the first Italian Catholic Church, Our Lady of Mount Carmel, was dedicated by Most Reverend Michael J. Hoban, Bishop of Scranton. For the first Sunday Mass, everyone was dressed in their best clothes and walked to 131 William Street. As the Italian parishioners of Our Lady of Mount Carmel walked by Saint John the Evangelist Church, they were greeted with women smiling and men tipping their hats.

As Maria, Rocco, and the children walked up the hill to church, they passed the large Pittston Stove building. There were large plumbs of smoke coming from the foundry. This building on 75 William street is one of the Wyoming Valley's oldest and most storied landmarks. On this site in the early 1860's, William Lister owned a foundry business, casting metal and iron products, known as Lister's Foundry. The tiny structure had succumbed to fire, and the property was sold by the sheriff in 1868 to a group of industrialists who formed a joint-stock company to conduct a larger foundry business. A charter was procured for the "Union Stove and Manufacturing Company" in 1869. One of the principal organizers and subsequent president was William N. Monies.

In 1868 Colonel Monies and Lewis Pugh purchased the Foundry Street property where Lister's Foundry once stood and began production in twenty different styles of coal and wood burning ranges. Following William Monies death in 1882, Union Stove was named "Pittston Stove Works."

Although the foundry was destroyed by fire, the large historic Pittston Stove building still stands today and is owned by Paul and Paula Caprari. They have preserved the building and historical artifacts. Currently it is the site of their Duchess Coat Outlet and began carrying women's and men's raincoats, wool jackets, leathers, and outerwear. Paula Caprari introduced Madame Alexander Dolls in 1984. In 2010 they opened a Doll Museum with over 1,000 dolls in the collection.

FIGURE. 14 PITTSTON STOVE WORKS (COURTESY JULIO CAPRARI)

As Rocco and Maria ascended to the top of the hill, they could see the cross on top of the church. Anthony Forlenza greeted everyone as they approached the property. He was proud the day finally arrived and Italian Catholics in Pittston would have their own church. The wooden church had six steps and double doors at the entrance. The organ played softly as Maria and Rocco and the family entered and genuflected before sitting in the pew. The beautiful white marble altar and tabernacle were crafted in Italy. Handmade white linens covering the altar were also made in Italy. On each side of the altar, there were smaller white marble altars with statutes of the Blessed Mother and Saint Joseph holding baby Jesus. Candles were lit on each altar providing a beautiful glow in the church.

The Knights of Columbus, Pittston Council 372, is one of the oldest in the country. Organized in 1898, there were sixty-six original charter members.

On this day, they stood on the sides of the altar and proudly served throughout the Mass. To this day, Council 372 exists as an important and influential force within the community and remains dedicated to providing charitable services.

The large polished wooden crucifix of Jesus adorned the wall behind the altar encased in a white marble cove. Kneeling in front was a statue of the Blessed Mother and her mother's sister Mary, the wife of Clopas, and Mary Magdalene. The wall behind it was covered with gold brocaded material trimmed in red. Bouquets of flowers throughout the church added to the very festive atmosphere. Most Reverend Michael J. Hoban blessed the church with holy water. Reverend William Gislon and Father John McLaughlin from Saint John the Evangelist Church assisted him at the Mass. Bishop Hoban spoke about the Italian heritage and their love for the Catholic church. Reverend Gislon was fluent in all Italian dialects and served this parish for many years.

After Mass Bishop Michael Hoban and Father Gislon greeted everyone as they entered the church basement. The parishioners enjoyed a social to get acquainted with each other. Coffee and Italian homemade pastries lined tables for everyone to enjoy. Different dialects echoed throughout the room. Some dressed in fine Italian silk clothing with leather shoes and purses; others wore the basic homemade cloth clothing customary from their part of Italy. Those from Rome, Naples, Perugia, and Umbria in northern Italy were trained in many different professions, such as carpenters, masons, tailors, bakers, and business owners. On the other hand, the southern Calabria region parishioners were farmers and laborers. Parishioners from the Island of Sicily were employed in the sulfur mines. Even though most settled in areas with Italian families from their region in Italy, all congregated and welcomed each other on Sunday.

The men from the San Cataldo Society, chartered in 1903, welcomed everyone and reached out to gain membership in their society from their fellow parishioners from San Cataldo, Italy. This rule was strictly adhered to because they had a special camaraderie with their fellow countrymen.

Some of the founding members of the church were Anthony Forlenza, a merchant in Pittston. He was instrumental in securing the land, planning and building of the church. Others included Joseph Sordoni, a counselor for the Italian people, Carl and Mary Solano, Pasquale and Marena Adonizio, Gennaro and Felicia Musto.

After the social, everyone left going in different directions depending on where they lived. As Rocco, Maria, and the children walked down the hill, on the other side of the street, they could see the four-story brick Pittston High School built in 1853.

As they continued on their way, they saw across from Saint John's Rectory, a large three-story brick residence. This home was owned by Michael Reap, who was a prominent pioneer resident of Pittston. He was engaged in the mercantile business and banking and served for a number of years as president of the Miners' Saving Bank. His home had many trees and finely trimmed bushes surrounding the porch, which was the full length of the structure. This corner property had a stone retaining wall running along William and Church streets, with a stairway on each side.

As they walked past Church Street, they could see the steeples from Saint Casimir's Church. The first Lithuanians arrived in Pittston in 1869. The Lithuanians were a very religious people, and their biggest concern was a Lithuanian Church and parish in the area to keep them and guide them in fulfilling their religious obligations.

In 1885 they formed the Saint Casimir's Beneficial Society, not only for their mutual help and guidance but to build a church and establish a parish. Soon three plots of land for the church and rectory were purchased at the cost of $1,931. The Lithuanians were determined to have their own church and parish, and on August 17th, 1886, a drive for more funds began.

A special delegation approached Bishop O'Hara of Scranton, seeking permission to establish a Lithuanian parish and build a church in Pittston. Permission was granted, and Bishop O'Hara promised to do his best to locate a Lithuanian priest for them. Although money was coming in at a slow pace, plans for the church building were completed. The digging of a cellar for the church 70'x40' was undertaken.

The cornerstone of the new church was blessed on June 30th, 1889 by Reverend John Finnen of Saint John's Church, Pittston. Preceding the blessing ceremony, there was a colorful parade.

In 1889 the church was completed and was blessed by Bishop O'Hara. He was assisted by Father A. Varnagiris, Father P. Abromavicus, and several other priests from the local churches. Some of the founding members were: Vincas Jasaitis (Sites), Andrius Teplusius, Andrius Klimavicius, Kazimeras Marcelonis, Jonas Balciunas, Peter Paul, and Anna Schevits Kashuba,

Although the Lithuanian people had their church, for some time they did not have a Lithuanian priest. There being no other Lithuanian priests available, Bishop O'Hara ordained a young priest, Father Juozas Zlotozinskas. In 1891 he was assigned to Saint Casimir's parish. Father Zlotozinskas, a most zealous priest, dedicated himself to the spiritual and material growth of the parish. In 1895 he developed pneumonia and died January 1896. In 1896 Father Michael Sedvodis was assigned to Saint Casmir's parish.

Due to an increase in the Lithuanian population, the church became too small for their needs. Soon the church was enlarged to accommodate 800 people. In January1895, the new church was blessed by Bishop O'Hara.

The Lithuanian Citizens' Social Beneficial Club was chartered on October 20th, 1913. The purpose for the corporation was the maintenance of a society for the mutual benefit or protection purposes as follows: providing funds collected from the members by initiation fees, monthly dues or fines, and the money realized to be paid out to such members thereof in case of sickness, accident, or death as shall be entitled thereto under the virtue of the by-laws.

At the top of Church Street, Rocco and Maria could see Saint Mary's Assumption (German) Church. The founding of Saint Mary's Assumption Church preceded the establishment of Pittston as a city by thirty-one years. The congregation was organized on October 1st, 1863, six weeks before President Abraham Lincoln delivered his famous Gettysburg Address during the height of the American Civil War. The parish was founded to serve the spiritual needs of a growing German population in the area. Between 1845 and 1885, scores of families left their native Germany to escape the harsh military government. These early immigrants found employment in the anthracite coal fields of Northeastern Pennsylvania and became a vital and contributing part of the community.

During these early years, without a church of their own, many early German families attended whatever church they could. Some attended Saint Mary's Church, the first Catholic Church in Pittston, which was erected on Chapel Street in the Junction section of Pittston in 1851. During these early years, Father Peter Nagel, a German priest and fellow immigrant, was sent by Bishop John Neumann, S.S.S.R., Bishop of Philadelphia, to shepherd the German Catholics in this region. Father Nagel visited Pittston several times each month to celebrate Mass and administer the Sacraments in private homes of the growing German community.

Following the founding of the congregation on October 1st, 1863, plans for the building of a church were advanced. The first church was built on land purchased from the Pennsylvania Coal Company at the lower north side of William Street, the former site of Saint John the Baptist (Slovak) Catholic Church. On September 4th, 1864, the cornerstone was laid, and Father Peter Nagel preached the dedicatory address. The first name of the Church was "The Roman Catholic Saint Peter's Church," named in honor of their beloved missionary priest, Fr. Peter Nagel. It was later changed to Saint Mary's Assumption Church.

The first resident pastor was Rev. Peter C. Christ. He was appointed by Bishop O'Hara on December 1st, 1883. During his brief tenure, the land for the parish cemetery in Hughestown was purchased. Although his tenure was brief, it was during this time that Saint Mary's Assumption School was formally established, and the first convent for the Sisters of Christian Charity was built. The need for a new school was recognized and ground was broken in October 1890 at the corner of Church and Sand streets. The Church was built on the corner of Church and Carroll streets in 1893. Father William Brehl broke ground, and the new structure was dedicated on January 1st, 1894.

As Maria, Rocco, and the children walked toward South Main Street, they soon reached the apartment. Sunday dinner was being prepared by Maria's mother, Victoria. It was a great day of celebration because of the opening of the first Italian Catholic Church. Cousins came over for dessert to celebrate this most important day.

As nightfall came, Maria and Rocco put the children to bed. Rocco kissed Maria and they fell asleep embraced in each other's arms. They knew it was time to move into their own apartment and wanted to be alone with their children. The following year, their fifth child, Joseph, was born.

Everyone was excited to hear that President Theodore Roosevelt was visiting the area. In August of 1905, President Theodore Roosevelt climbed into a carriage at the River Common after a triumphant day in Wilkes-Barre where he was regaled by hundreds of thousands of adoring coalminers, laborers, clerks, professional men and their families. The crowd was estimated at 200,000 with 80,000 being coalminers.

Four Secret Service agents on horses led the president's six-carriage party over the Market Street Bridge to Kingston. Wilkes-Barre Mayor Fred Kirkendall and United Miner Workers President John Mitchell rode in the lead carriage with the president. The president's son, nephew, cousin and doctor rode in the second, followed by carriages of labor leaders and clergy. On Wyoming Avenue, the president's driver whipped the horses to a fast trot and the crowds lining the sidewalks in Kingston and Forty Fort got only a glimpse of the carriage as it hurried, behind schedule, toward the Wyoming Monument. Carriages, farmers' horses, and even automobiles lined the avenue for a mile in each direction.

The mines and shops in Wyoming, West Pittston, and Pittston closed at noon. In West Pittston and Exeter, the West Side electric cars couldn't handle demand for fares to the monument. In Pittston the Laurel Line – the Scranton-to-Wilkes-Barre commuter line—ran double sections to Wilkes-Barre every five minutes. But even at that, thousands were left on the platform as the cars were nearly filled when they got to Pittston.

When the President arrived at the monument, he was covered with dust. He hadn't eaten since lunch on the train and was worn out by the seven-hour train trip, a thirty-minute speech in the August sun in Wilkes-Barre and the endless crowds and well-wishers. The President read the inscription on the monument and met Zebulon Butler, a fifth-generation descendant of Colonel Zebulon Butler, the commander with Nathan Denison, of the colonials at the Battle of Wyoming.

"My boy," Roosevelt said to Butler, "you are the right kind of Colonial stock and I'm glad to meet you."

Back in his carriage, the President asked if there was a way to avoid going back to Wilkes-Barre. The Pittston station was only three miles. A wire was sent to the train in Wilkes-Barre. When the President's carriage left the monument and turned north on Wyoming Avenue toward Exeter, citizens in carriages and horseback played Paul Revere, racing ahead by side street to Pittston, yelling, "The President is coming."

Few knew what was happening in Exeter or West Pittston. At the Water Street Bridge, toll taker W.H. Young was one of the non-believers until four Secret Service agents on horseback galloped to the gate and identified themselves. Young waved the President and his party through. Theodore "Teddy" Harris, a young boy from Laceyville, and Harriet Hitchner of the famous bakery family were on the bridge with some other boys.

They ran as close to the carriage as they could get with Harris yelling, "I'm named for you." The president told the driver to stop, so he could shake hands with his namesake. When Roosevelt told the boy to make his mother and father proud, the boy said, "I don't have a father."

Roosevelt said, "That's too bad, then make the President proud."

The agents, deputies, and Pittston police took the President into the train station. Citizens already in the station were allowed to stay to meet the President, but the doors were closed. The Secret Service agents commandeered the ladies waiting room where Roosevelt rested and greeted some of the city's "leading citizens." The crowd of about 5,000 chanted for a speech. When the conductor pulled the bell card for the start signal, the president stepped onto the rear platform and waved to the crowd. He stayed on the platform waving to people who lined the tracks for three miles to Coxton. At that time, he returned to his quarters.

The next day, when Maria went to buy flour to make bread, she saw cousin Michael and his son Francesco crossing the street. They greeted each other and began to talk about the President's visit to Pittston the previous day. It was one of the most exciting events they experienced since their move to America. During their conversation, Michael told Maria there was an apartment available near him on Johnson Street in the Oregon section of Pittston. When Rocco came home from work, she told him about the apartment for rent on Johnson Street. The next day, they went to see the owner and put a deposit on the apartment.

*Chapter 10*

## MOVE TO OREGON SECTION
## AND SOUTHERN ITALIAN IMMIGRATION

The vast majority of Italians in Oregon, Railroad Street, and Pine Street came from the former Independent and Sovereign State of Southern Italy, the Kingdom of the Two Sicilies. It included all continental southern Italy from Abruzzi, to Calabria and Puglia, and Sicily. They settled close to each other because their Italian language, dialect, and foods were different from northern Italians. The northern Italians settled in the Pittston Township area known as Cork Lane. They had a special Italian club erected on Poole Street for meetings and social gatherings. Even though northern Italians and southern Italians had differences, they were very respectful of each other and their customs.

Oregon was two blocks from South Main Street. In the 1800's, it was a forest with all types of trees and bushes. Most of the land was owned by Colonel James Johnson. Also, William Tompkins had a large farm located in this area. Both men were early settlers in Pittston and were instrumental in forming the roads and designing Main Street as it still is today. Adjoining this area was Mr. Swallow's farm.

To recognize these first settlers, the roads were named in their honor. Oregon has five large main streets: Elizabeth, Tompkins, Johnson, River, and Oak. Near River Street, there is a park called Burke Park in honor of a serviceman killed in World War I and was also known as Oregon Grove. Although many Italians lived in this area, there were also Irish, Lithuanian, and Polish immigrants. Some of the families living in this area were Scarantino, Brogna, Amico, Mastruzzo, Paragis, Burns, Scot, Connor, Murphy and Manganaro.

Lorenzo and Mary Grace Brogna had a corner grocery store, however, it was called Mrs. Brown's because people couldn't pronounce their name. Rizzo's had a Butcher Shop. Leonardi's had a grocery store on Tompkins Street. Mullen's had a candy store on Johnson Street.

At the summit of Oregon, Pittston Hospital, called the Miners' Hospital, opened on November 1st, 1893 on four acres of land donated by the Pittston Coal Company. With many collieries in Pittston, it was built to take care of injured miners. The first superintendent was Mr. John Gibson. Dr. Michael Underwood was Chief-of-Staff.

The main three-story brick building was situated in the center. On each end were two wooden structures with each ward containing thirty-two beds. It soon became apparent that accidents at home involving women and children, and childbirth were reasons to enlarge the hospital. In 1903 the Pittston Hospital School of Nursing opened with Ms. Helen Castro the first Director of Nursing. With the growing population in Pittston and surrounding areas, the hospital soon expanded to accommodate more patients.

Although Maria and Rocco enjoyed living with family when they arrived in Pittston, they were anxious to have their own apartment. Soon a new chapter of their lives would begin in a different part of Pittston. They gathered their belongings and walked to the Oregon section.

Rocco, Maria, and the five children arrived at 121 Johnson Street. After speaking with the owner, they entered the apartment. It was a black wooden structure similar to other apartments and homes in the area. The apartment had four rooms, two downstairs and two upstairs.

It was very old and needed repairs and cleaning. To get a cheaper rent, Rocco assured the owner that he could make the needed repairs. As they walked in the door, there was a table with four chairs left by the previous owner.

The coal/wood stove worked but needed to be cleaned. In a short period of time, Rocco and Carlo had the stove working. The family helped with getting food provisions and used furniture. There was a wooden tub for bathing, but the water had to be carried in buckets from the water provided by the city from a central street location. The water had to be heated on the stove for bathing. Clean water was always held in jugs for drinking.

There was no indoor bathroom, but outhouses were located on each street. Every family was respectful of one another and allowed for privacy at all times. Chamber pots were in the house to be used during the night hours. Cousin Michael and his son Francesco brought candles and an old railroad lantern for light. Many cousins brought food to welcome them to Oregon.

Maria and Victoria were busy making blankets and rugs to keep the floors warm and the beds cozy. Rosa and Michael ran around and explored their new home going up and down the stairs.

They were so happy in their new apartment. It was a busy day, and in the evening, everyone was exhausted and fell asleep quickly. Rocco had to get up early to work in the coal mine.

As Rocco walked home from work, he noticed wild flowers growing in an open field nearby. He picked some and surprised Maria with a small bouquet to put in the center of the table. She was so excited when he walked through the door with the wild flowers and gave them to her with a wide smile. It brought back memories of the flowers he would pick for her in Italy. After the children were asleep, Rocco and Maria caressed each other. Their love was evident by the way they treated each other with respect and love. Having their own apartment was a big accomplishment, and they worked hard to repair it and make a loving home for their children. She was the one he adored, and he knew it the day he saw her at the church. He caressed her body, and they fell asleep holding each other. They welcomed their sixth child Carlo the following year.

After a long, hard week of work, it was finally Sunday. Almost all nationalities attended church services. This Sunday Rocco, Maria, and the children made a much longer walk to Our Lady of Mount Carmel Church. They passed the lower end of Railroad Street filled with people of many different nationalities walking to church. They passed Pine Street where many Italians from Serradifalco lived. They wanted to live in close proximity of each other when they came to America. Serradifalco was a town in Sicily located in close proximity of San Cataldo. These immigrants previously worked in the sulfur mines in Sicily. They were experienced laborers and were able to advance in the sulfur mining industry. The Serradifalco Society celebrates the feast of its patron saint, Our Lady of Sorrows, on the third Sunday of September. The celebration commemorates a tragedy turned miracle, which took place in the little town of Serradifalco. A gas explosion occurred in a sulfur mine. This mine employed most of the men of the town. The people rushed into their church and lifted the statue of Our Lady of Sorrows onto their shoulders and carried it to the opening of the mine shaft. With the people on their knees, they prayed for a miracle. Before long, as the miners made their way out of the mineshaft, they saw the statue of Our Lady of Sorrows with the people of the town praying in front of it. The miners made their way to the statue and draped the cape of the statue around their bodies for shelter. Nearly all of the miners made it to safety. The members of the Serradifalco Society of Pittston have honored the statue of Our Lady of Sorrows with a feast day.

The hill going from Railroad Street was called Welsh Hill. This area was inhabited by some of the Welsh residents in Pittston. On the top of the hill, located at 40 LaGrange Street, was the Welsh Congregational Church. This church had fifty members of Welsh descent. The Evans family was part of the founding members. The church wasn't in existence for a long period of time because the building was destroyed by mine subsidence.

In the 19th century, thousands of Welsh coal miners immigrated to the anthracite and bituminous mines of Pennsylvania, many becoming mine managers and executives. They were hard workers and very experienced in mining.

The Welsh Baptist Church, constructed at 42 LaGrange Street, was organized in 1851. In October of that year, the church was received into the Baptist Organization, which then included the territory between Carbondale and Pittston. The first pastor was Ebenezer Edwards. Although Pastor Edwards served for only one year, the church was fondly referred to as the "Ebenezer Church." The first place of worship was Battles Hall, located on the corner of South Main and Charles Street. There were fifty-two initial members. During the first year, a building was erected on the corner of Oak and LaGrange streets.

At least ten preachers commanded the pulpit between 1851 and 1891. In 1892, Reverend William D. Thomas was called to service, and the church thrived under his guidance. In 1905 he was instrumental in the erection of an addition to the church edifice. As the years went by, nearly all of the Welsh speaking members had passed away. Membership was in decline, and a special business meeting was held to discuss the possible merger with another Baptist church in Pittston. It was decided to merge with the First Baptist Church on Water Street. Later the Ebenezer property was sold to the Italian Christian Pentecostal Church. Reverend Julio Caprari became pastor and remained active in the church until his passing. The Italian Christian Church continues to prosper in this location under Reverend Peter Caprari.

As they neared the corner of William Street, they could see the grand opening sign on the Flat Iron Building. Mr. Joseph J. Sordoni organized the first private bank in Pittston. This bank was located at 40 North Main Street. In 1907 this bank moved to the Flat Iron Building.

Upon arriving in the United States between 1890 and 1920, large numbers of sulfur miners settled in Pittston, Dunmore, and Old Forge. Although they were strong supporters of the 1902 strike and John Mitchell, they soon began to leave the union out of dissatisfaction with its conservative leadership and policies. By 1905 they were collaborating with militant workers from other ethnic groups in a series of wildcat strikes. In 1907 the Industrial Workers of the World (IWW) began organizing in the northern anthracite field, and the Italians at Pennsylvania Coal Company and Hillside Coal and Iron Company were among the most receptive to the union's philosophy.

Once in the United States, where they were free of many old-world constraints, they stood at the forefront in organizing Italian and other immigrants in demanding better pay and working conditions.

Although the Italians on strike in 1907 had legitimate grievances and wanted to make a better life for their families, many were seen as belonging to gangs and creating violent disturbances.

The "Black Hand" was a group of men determined to extort money from wealthy Italians and other nationalities. If their demands were not met, they would use intimidation tactics.

Because of the inference of violence, many Italians formed the White Hand Society. This society was formed by law-abiding Sons of Italy who were determined to overcome the stereotypes perpetuated by the criminal element. Their mission was to do good deeds and help others in all aspects of life.

# *Chapter 11*

## BROAD STREET

After church on Sunday, Maria and Rocco took the children to the park located on Broad Street. As they reached the corner of Broad and Main Street, builders were putting the finishing touch on the sign for the F. W. Woolworth Five and Ten Cent Store. This store was built on the site of the former Cash Store Block. Two brothers, Frank Winfield Woolworth, and his brother, Charles Sumner Woolworth, started their store chain in New York and soon expanded to Wilkes-Barre and Scranton. In 1907 this store opened in Pittston.

Consolidated Telephone Company was at 4 Broad Street. John Scrimgeour Plumbing was across the street at 5 Broad Street, and attorney Harold J. Mahon had his sign at 6 Broad Street.

As they passed the First Presbyterian Church, parishioners offered them a free cup of soup. They accepted graciously and were welcomed by this congregation. They had small cups of warm milk for the children.

Across the street from the church at 7 Broad Street was the German Kitchen, owned by four young German sisters, Bertha, Regina, Rose, and Anna Dommermuth. It boasted fine home cooking and was a way the girls could support themselves and their aging parents. They were listed in the "Black Diamond Cook Book" as the "German Kitchen," 7 Broad Street, second-floor, Dinner 11 to 2, supper 5:30 to 7:00, lunch served to order, Dommermuth Sisters Proprietor. The German Kitchen flourished for a number of years. It enjoyed a well-earned reputation for fine home-cooked food, and it catered to the business tradesmen. It also served banquets for well-known organizations. The sisters covered their tables with spotless white linen tablecloths and used large linen dinner napkins. At the entrance was a small white finger bowl with warm water for customers to cleanse their fingers before eating.

The United Methodist Church, established in 1849, built their church at the corner of Church and Broad streets. It had a beautiful stone and brick exterior. On the roof, the large grey wooden cupola looked like a small grey house with windows. Inside near the altar was a large oak pipe organ that could be heard as people walked by. The church's mission statement: To reach out to people in the name of Jesus Christ, relating them to God, to nurture and strengthen them in our journey of discipleship and go into the world to be the Church of God, welcoming others to join us on their journey.

Across from the church was a large open grassy park. As they entered the park, many pretty colored flowers and bushes were along the pathway. It made them feel as if they were entering a beautiful garden. Children played games and swung high on the swings. A circular shaped roofed bandshell was used for speeches and other announcements. For sunny days, there were seats to rest in this area. People of all nationalities enjoyed the park on this warm Sunday afternoon. Soon it would turn colder and school would be in session. Boys threw balls while girls jumped rope. Others drew on the dirt with a stick for a game of hop-scotch. Everyone was friendly and the children smiled and welcomed other children to play. The park was a place to meet families from other nationalities and to learn English from other families.

The "Peoples Light Company" was located at 15 Broad Street, and at 19 Broad Street was the Broad Street Theater and Opera House. The theater was opened on September 7th, 1903. Outstanding road shows, including some of the greatest minstrel performers of the day, played at this theater. It was also the scene of many local amateur shows and minstrels, including the Stellar Minstrel productions directed by Thomas J. Hennigan. The name was changed to the Princess Theater, and still later it became known as the Strand Theater. This theater operated for some time as a movie house, prior to its eventual closing as a place of entertainment.

At 54-56 Broad Street was a large three-story building with different levels and heights. This was a grain store. Later this building was used for many years by Radio City-Pittston Appliance and was owned by Harry Mertz.

Next door was a large two-story grey building used as a pumping station for the mines. Men worked in shifts pumping water from the mines into the river. It was in operation twenty-four hours a day. This was dangerous work, and at times there were fatalities.

The Methodist Protestant Church was built at 66 Broad Street with Pastor, Reverend J. Hudson. Its church and Sunday School membership was small in number. In later years, it closed and joined with the United Methodist Church. Today it is the site of the Perspective Church with Reverend Samuel Washington.

As Rocco and Maria looked up Broad Street, they could see large piles of beautiful pink and grey Belgium cobblestones that were going to be laid on Foundry Street. In the years to come, all of the downtown area had these beautiful cobble stones.

While Maria, Rocco, and the children walked home to Oregon, they could see the men working on the State Armory, erected in 1907, at the corner of South Main and Swallow streets. It was the home of Pennsylvania National Guard. Social activities, banquets, and large mass meetings were held in its spacious drill hall. This building still stands today.

The first amusement tax was enacted in Pittston in 1907, when it became law that clubs and associations must obtain a permit to conduct dances. There were many local bands and dancing was a popular recreation. Many establishments catered to this pastime and provided a large dance floor. The Keating Brothers were a well-known band and made a living for many years as younger generations became members of the band.

Joseph H. Glennon purchased the Central Park plot at 457 North Main Street, Pittston, the former site of the home of Nathaniel Giddings. Work on the excavation for the foundation of Glennon's brewery began in January 4th, 1907. The structure was completed and started as a brewery the following year. It was advertised at that time as the most modern brewery in the world. On August 8th, 1908, a huge double electric sign containing 800 bulbs was placed on the building and was lighted. On Saturday, December 12th, 1908, this brewery was referred to as the only brewery in the world entirely equipped with electricity.

As Maria walked home, she started going into labor. A kind gentleman with a horse and buggy drove the family to the Pittston Hospital. Dr. Underwood, who was working in the emergency room, soon attended to Maria. By the end of the day, their seventh child, Laura, was born. They were elated with the safe birth and thanked the kind nurses for letting the children in the room to see their baby sister.

After two weeks, Maria was released from the hospital. Her mother, Victoria, stayed with the family to help take care of the children. All of the neighbors in Oregon Section were caring and friendly to each other. Whenever there was a family in need of help, the neighbors assisted them. Soon after Maria was home from the hospital, their neighbor Joe Paragis came over with eggs, vegetables, and fresh milk from his cow. The children loved to visit him because he would let them milk the cow and pick the eggs from the straw beneath the chickens. He had a large piece of land on Johnson Street and shared his food with his neighbors.

Soon school would be in session, and Rosa would attend the Cleveland School around the corner from their house. Maria and Rosa walked to the Main Street to purchase a pair of shoes for

Rosa's first day of school. Rocco and Maria saved some change from every paycheck to make this purchase. Maria and Rosa walked to Main Street and passed several shoe stores along the way. The prices of the shoes were higher than Maria had expected. Rosa saw a red pair of shoes in the window of Mr. Louis Schiffman's store. As they were looking at them in the window, Louis Schiffman came out on the sidewalk and greeted them with a smile.

Maria expressed concern over the price of the shoes and Louis Schiffman replied, "Come in the store to see if the shoe would fit Rosa." He told Maria not to worry about the cost of the shoes. He was trying to explain to Maria that she could buy on credit and pay for the shoes a little at a time. She did not understand what he was trying to explain. At that moment, Angelo Sciandra was walking home from working in the mines. He overheard Louis Schiffman and he explained in Italian to Maria what he was saying.

She was astonished at this proposal and said she would have to ask her husband, Rocco, before she would agree to this transaction. When Rocco came home from work, she explained to him how they were going to pay for the shoes, and Rocco agreed to accept this kind offer to purchase the shoes. He was surprised by this and went to the store the next day to talk to Louis Schiffman. He shook Louis Schiffman's hand, and they became friends from that day forward. When Maria and Rocco went to make a payment on the shoes, they were told a gentleman came in and paid for all of the children's shoes that were in the unpaid book register.

A tradition of mutual respect and assistance existed among Jews and Gentiles in Pittston. The tradition endured through the years when Jews, most of them proprietors of small stores, performed a real service for the miners by providing alternatives to high priced company stores and by allowing payments to slide during strikes, mine closings, and work lulls.

Pittson was a very religious community, and many Jewish merchants also made Pittson their home. The Jewish Congregation worshiped in a wooden house at 60 Broad Street. This became inadequate to meet the needs of the growing congregation of sixty families, and architect Turon was asked to draw plans for a new building. The Wolden house was moved to the rear of the property to be used by visiting clercy. Temple Agudath Achim, a new wood-sided synagogue, seating 250, was opened in May 1916 at 60 Broad Street. Although remodeled with a red brick exterior, this building stands today.

On Sunday Rocco, Maria, and the children walked to church with many other Italians from their area. Our Lady of Mount Carmel Church was a distance from Oregon, especially in the winter months.

As they ascended the hill to the Italian church, they passed Defoe Street, which crossed with Butler Street. Many German families lived in this area and were walking to Saint Mary's Church on the top of Church Street.

In the beginning of 1909, Rocco and Maria were blessed with their eighth child, Frank. It was a difficult birth, and the underweight baby boy wasn't breathing. At that point, Dr. Underwood cleared the baby's throat and massaged his chest to get the baby to breathe. In a few minutes, the baby was crying. Father Gislon, who was called to the hospital to baptize little Frank, stayed all night at the hospital with Rocco and Maria. The next day, Frank improved, but he had to stay in the hospital in a special warming area. When his lungs developed, he would be able to leave the hospital. The doctors were very concerned with his deteriorating condition. Maria and Rocco were very upset that they could possibly lose Frank. Father Gislon visited every day. After a month, Frank was able to go home with the instructions he was to be kept warm.

Rocco and Maria made a special small wooden crib and placed homemade blankets in it to keep him covered. He was kept at the side of the coal stove to be warm at all times until he gained weight. They had to take him to Dr. Underwood's office every week for the first two months of his life. In six months, Dr. Underwood said his lungs were developed and considered him healthy.

At the end of 1909, they were blessed with their ninth child, Rocco. He had beautiful black hair and brown eyes. They were happy they had a large and healthy family.

Pittston and its outlying areas were in turmoil on March 2nd, 1909, when a serious explosion occurred at about eight o'clock in the morning at the No.14 shaft of the Pennsylvania Coal Company. It was, however, not until noon that the exact result of the explosion, so far as it affected the lives of workmen, was known. In those few hours, anxiety prevailed throughout the city and surrounding towns.

The explosion occurred soon after the colliery started operation for the day, and as in all mine accidents, the news spread like wildfire in downtown Pittston. Because a fire followed the explosion, it was impossible at once to penetrate that part of the workings where the trouble occurred, and the wildest rumors were afloat. For hours it was believed that fifty mine workers were behind a raging wall of fire in the mine.

The gloom and anxiety of the waiting crowd at the colliery, on the streets of Pittston and in the homes of the people, turned to comparative gladness when, as the noon hour neared, the rescuers and firefighters got the upper hand on the flames that raged in the affected slope. It was learned for certain that only a couple of workmen remained in the immediate vicinity of the fire and met death there. When underground workers heard the roar of the explosion, they immediately made their way out of the workings. Unfortunately rescuers found two victims. These two, in addition to thirteen men who had been removed from the mine soon after the rescuers started work who were caught at the edge of the fiery flame, comprised all of the victims of the explosion.

Investigators learned that all of the trouble was located in the Pittston vein, which was the largest and best vein in No.14 colliery. The coal, thick and of excellent quality, for many years had been the chief source of supply of the Pennsylvania Coal Company. It was one of the veins chiefly relied on to furnish coal for the big breaker that prepared the product of No. 14 for the market.

Later investigators discovered that a miner went into the old workings with a bare carbide lamp. There was a large accumulation of dangerous gas there which was ignited by the naked carbide lamp, with the resulting force of a terrific explosion. Sadly mine accidents resulting in injuries and sometimes death were a way of life in all mining communities.

A large number of Polish people lived in the Oregon section. They appealed to the Bishop to build a church for them to practice their religion. The Polish people brought with them their great work ethic but also their devotion to the Catholic faith and their ethnic customs. On November 7th, 1909, the first Mass was celebrated for the Parish of Saint Joseph by Father Ladislaus Ziemianski in the newly constructed church, which was located at the top of Elizabeth Street. Soon land was secured on River Street in Oregon Heights for a Polish cemetery.

In 1909 plans were made to erect a bank on the northwestern corner of Water and Main streets. It was named the Peoples Union Savings Bank. The land where the bank was to be built was an empty lot that had trees and brush and was known at that time as "The Green." Also, in 1909, the automobile was introduced in Pittston, when Stroh Brothers became agents for the Regal Automobile Company.

Woodlawn Dairy, Purvin Dairy, and Renna Dairy used horse drawn wagons to deliver their products. Also, coal deliveries and all types of freight made their way around the city and to outlying towns by horse drawn wagons. Mr. J.O.D. Mangan, who operated a bakery and general store, had a stable on East Railroad Street, where he kept his horses and wagons used in his businesses.

Giuseppe and Justina Augello had a grocery store and butcher shop on South Main Street. In the window, Mr. Augello could be seen trimming the meat and placing it on display. They were known for their delicious tomato sauce and had a sign in the window advertising Italian Spaghetti. The Augello family is still in business as the Gramercy restaurant at 155 South Main Street.

Life was not easy for the average coal mining family. Fruits and vegetables planted in the gardens were canned for the winter months. Winters were especially hard because the family had to keep coal in the stove for heat. Many women with their children would go to the culm banks and look for pieces of coal for the stoves. If a miner was killed in a mining accident or for any other reason, the women and children in the apartments had to find a way to pay the rent. Sometimes if a miner was killed in the mines, the body would be put on the porch with a knock on the door for the family to discover their loved one. Sometimes the deceased miner's family was notified and given a ton of coal. After that if a family did not have another source of income to pay their rent, they were told by the landlord to find other means of shelter.

The churches and the parishioners with more wealth were always there for families in need. If family members put their name on a list, they would be helped. At times, when the mine wasn't working for some reason, there was no choice but to ask for help. Also, when needed The White Hand Society was there for families.

One morning when Maria was coming back from getting water, she saw some men from the church putting bags of coal near her door. One of the men was Pasquale (Tony Rose) Adonizio. He was always a caring and helpful person to everyone. Later in life, he had his own coal company and hired everyone in need of a job. He was especially kind to his employees. He was presented with a marble bust of his likeness. His employees contributed for the four-foot high green marble pedestal with the bust on top. It was the work of Onorio Rutolo, sculptor from New York City.

# Chapter 12

## THE ROOSEVELT SCHOOL AND SPEAKEASIES

Theodore Roosevelt, former President of the United States, made a surprise visit to Pittston on August 3rd, 1910, accompanied by Reverend John J. Curran of Wilkes-Barre, with whom he spent the previous day, and John Mitchell International President of the United Mine Workers of America. While here the distinguished visitor inspected the Roosevelt School at South Pittston. This recently completed school was named in his honor. In front of a large crowd, the former President thanked the City of Pittston for the honor of having the new school named after him. He made many visits to Luzerne County and outlying areas when he was the President of the United States. The coal miners were always in his heart as the bravest men whose tedious and dangerous work fueled the Industrial Revolution.

Many of the coal miners in the crowd listening and clapping for the President had blackened faces and just finished their shift in the mines. Others were on their way to work in a coal mine. Sadly young male children on their fathers' shoulders were also going to a coal mine to work in a coal breaker. They applauded after every sentence and showed the President how much respect and honor they had for him, Father John J. Curran, and John Mitchell.

The reception President Roosevelt received throughout his two days among the miners was pleasing to him. By automobile he covered more than 150 miles of rough mountain roads, visited dozens of miners' homes, and was saluted with dynamite explosions. Just as remarkable as the President's reception was the one accorded John Mitchell.

This was not an unusual occurrence for John Mitchell, the President of the United Mine Workers of America. As the visitors left Duryea, they passed a miner sitting in a rocking chair asleep on the porch of a saloon. This was a very common sight in the coal towns of northeastern Pennsylvania. By the time he was awakened by the tavern owner, former President Roosevelt, John Mitchell, and Father Curran were in the car and on their way. After a hard day of work in a coal mine, it didn't matter what shift the miners were working, many would stop at their favorite local tavern.

Duryea, Dupont, and Exeter all had thirty to forty bars each and there were ninety-one bars in Pittston. Many were in the proprietors' living rooms. There were thirty-three bars on North Main Street, seven in the 600 block, and thirty-nine on South Main Street. The Miners' Bar at 38 South Main was dubbed the Squib Box by patrons because it was only seven feet wide.

Although the coal industry was one of the most lucrative businesses in the small coal mining towns, beer manufacturers and liquor distributors were the second source of substantial revenue.

Tobacco use was also prevalent with coal miners. In every block of Pittston City, there were many stores selling cigars, cigarettes, and chewing tobacco.

The winter of 1910 was very harsh with many snow storms. Streets were filled with snow, and the city workers tried their best to clear the streets and make them passable. It was difficult to get water and food and many families depended on their homemade canned goods to survive the winter. Joe Paragis used his car to deliver food to neighbors in need. When Rocco came home from the mines, he helped him deliver food to some of the neighbors in Oregon.

When Rocco returned home, Maria had the house warm and the children were sleeping. Maria was pregnant, and the sight of her body made Rocco caress and cuddle her. Sometimes they would just lay there and talk about their lives in America. Although they missed the warm weather in southern Italy, America was their dream come true, even though winters were hard in Pennsylvania. They struggled to provide everything for their family, but it was all worth it.

On February 6th, 1911, a severe blow to illegal liquor traffic was dealt by the Pittston City police department when Chief of Police Price conducted well-planned raids on alleged speakeasies on many streets in the city. The city police force was assisted by Lieutenant Marsh, of the Pennsylvania State Police, and fifteen troopers. At least fifteen locations were raided, and a number of men were arrested and a large quantity of liquor confiscated. At city hall, a police court was held for owners of the speakeasies and all kind of excuses were given on why the illegal booze was on the premises.

One man said, "He kept the booze on his property for his friends, and he never charges for the drinks."

Another said, "He was a brewery collector and went into the place to collect a bill."

It was a common sight to see the shiny five gallon cans containing alcohol, brought into the cellars of homes where illegal stills were in operation in south Pittston. South Main street between Market and Oak streets had a few backroom wine shops. The grapes to make the wine sold in Pittston came in refrigerated freight cars. The cars were placed on a side of the Lehigh Valley Railroad behind their freight house on Water Street. The operation of illegal stills and wine making was a usual practice in south Pittston.

The landscape of Pittston was changing, and the temporary management of the new Dime Bank had decided to avail itself the option to purchase the Streng lot on the west side of South Main Street opposite Charles Street to erect a modern bank building. The lot purchased had a frontage of twenty-five feet and the depth of 120 feet. The Pittston Dime Bank and Trust Company, built by John J. Reilly, opened on July 1st, 1911, with assets worth $57,795, at 29 South Main Street, across from Charles Street. Construction of this bank changed the landscape of downtown Pittston.

Although Pittston was changing, the struggles for the miners continued. The Salvatore Valenti family came to the United States in 1911. Their son Rosario (Ross) Valenti was eleven-years-old and became a mule driver in the mines. Ross was small for his age and looked younger than his years. One day, when he was alone in the mine, he got off the mule and was between the mule and the wall of coal. The mule started to squeeze him against the wall of coal. He could not move and was being crushed with no one around to help him. He knew he didn't have long to live, and the only thing he could think of doing to save himself was to bite down hard on the mule's back. It worked and he was released. When he came home from work, still looking frightened and afraid, his mother asked him what happened.

He told his mother," I was almost killed by the mule, and I feel like I left my childhood in Italy."

On June 5th, 1911, a mine explosion resulted in the tragic deaths of Walter Fitzsimmons, a young man from Inkerman, Pennsylvania, and Martin C. Quinn, a well- known resident of Nafus Street in Pittston. Fitzsimmons was killed instantly and Quinn died later at Pittston Hospital.

The death of Fitzsimmons was extremely sad. He was unmarried, twenty-two-years-old, and resided with his aunt, Mrs. James Cooney, on Shaft Street, Inkerman. He was in good spirits previous to leaving the house to go to work. He walked to the shaft, which was within sight of the Cooney home. Within a half hour, word came to the Cooney family that he had met death while working in the mine.

Fitzsimmons was employed as a mule driver in No. 11 shaft, Pennsylvania Coal Company. After descending the shaft, he was traveling along the gangway only a short distance from the foot of the shaft when the explosion occurred. Mine officials theorized that a pocket of gas accumulated on the gangway and that Fitzsimmons, who was carrying a naked lamp, ignited the gas.

Only a half hour before the accident, Fire Boss John Williams had passed through the gangway on his inspection tour and reported that everything was all right. It was said at that time that there was generally very little gas in No. 11 mine and that it is unusual to find gas close to the foot of the shaft. The fan at No. 5 shaft, however, was undergoing repairs and the fan had been stopped for a few hours. Inside Foreman Tom Madden of No. 11 was on duty all day before the gas explosion. He said he stayed until eight o'clock in the evening and personally went through the mine to be sure that the air currents were in good condition after the fan had resumed operating.

Martin C. Quinn of Pittston died from his injuries incurred in the No. 11 shaft explosion of 1911. At the time of the explosion, he was working as a company inside man. He was sitting on an electric motor in the mine waiting to be taken to his work when the explosion occurred. He was on the edge of the explosion and escaped being burned by the flames but was struck by a heavy mine door that was blown off by the explosion. It was thought at that time that his injuries were not serious and hope was entertained for his recovery, but he gradually weakened and succumbed to his injuries.

Rocco and Frank were walking home from their shift at No. 6 coal mine when they saw some miners walking home from the Ewen breaker. They immediately recognized a very large husky man coming towards them. As he came closer, they realized it was their good neighbor and friend from Italy, Gregorio (Billy) Paglianite. He did not recognize them because of their coal dust blackened faces. As they yelled to him in Italian, he remembered their voices and answered immediately. It was a joyous reunion. Billy said he was living in the Cork Lane section of Pittston Township, close by another good friend from Italy, Joseph Ranieli. They made plans to visit each other in the near future.

In the spring of 1911, Maria and Rocco welcomed their tenth child, Anthony. He was a chubby baby boy with long eyelashes and wavy hair. Soon two other Policare cousins were born, Joe and Maggie. When they were baptized together at Our Lady of Mount Carmel Church by Father Gislon, a large family party was held on the street near their home in Oregon. They invited their dear friends from Italy. Billy Paglianite married Anna Aruzzo, and Joseph Ranieli married her sister Mary. Everyone had a joyous time and talked about their memories of Italy. America was their "new" homeland and everyone realized there would be more opportunity for future generations.

Rocco and Maria's oldest son, Michael, applied for a job at Antonio Restuccio's fruit and confection store located at 99 South Main Street. He was happy to be selected and started working after school and on Saturdays loading the fruit from the railroad car into the wagons and up the street to the store. Also, he would help set up the displays and cleaning the store. Dominick, his brother, worked for the Corcoran Brothers, as a shoeshine boy inside their store after school and on Saturdays. The boys were happy to help their family and kept a small portion of their earnings for themselves.

Maria's neighbor, Giuseppe (Joe) Tuminello, needed help with his children when his wife, Lucia, went into pre-mature labor. Because of this emergency, Maria watched their children with hers and made them feel welcome. Giuseppe, Jr., just fourteen-years-old, entertained everyone with playing his trumpet. He could always be heard practicing his trumpet after school. With the help of Joseph Paragis, Michael and Lucia arrived at Pittston Hospital at the top of Johnson Street. As they reached the entrance, they were met by Miss Esther Tinsley. In August of 1913, Miss Tinsley became administrator of the Pittston Hospital and its nursing school. Miss Tinsley, a native of Plymouth, Pennsylvania, and the oldest of seven children, was a graduate of Saint Mary's Academy in 1902, and The University of Pennsylvania nursing school in 1910.

After working for a short period of time at Nesbitt Hospital, Miss Tinsley accepted a position at Pittston Hospital.

Miss Tinsley immediately called for a gurney to transport Lucia to the birthing area. Dr. Underwood was in the hospital at the time and assisted in the difficult birth. A few hours later, Miss Tinsley let the family know that a beautiful, under-weight, healthy baby boy was born and that Lucia was doing fine.

In 1914 S.S.Kresge Company opened a 5 and 10 cent store at 9 North Main Street, next door to Woolworth's store. Its front sign was a bright red color, and inside they had a counter where customers could sit on stools to have a soda or ice cream. This was a new novelty in Pittston and gathered a large crowd every Saturday. The week before Christmas, they gave away, to all families, a silver star for the top of their Christmas tree.

During this week, the family put up a small evergreen tree that Rocco found in a field. They placed it in a bucket with water and rocks to secure it. Rocco and Maria topped the tree with the star they received at Kresge's store and placed a string with different color beads around the tree. The children hung home-made paper ornaments of different colors on the branches. After church on Christmas Day, they went to Carlo and Victoria's house for a home-made pasta dinner and dessert.

Everyone in Pittston was excited when the Roman Theater opened in 1914 at 27 South Main Street. There was seating for 700. It was very popular, and the following year, another 300 seats were added.

Pittston was changing; streets were being paved, sanitary sewers laid, and the city was being electrified. Most of the streets were wired for electricity, but many homeowners were not hooked up, more because of fear than cost. Despite the improvements, life was dangerous and dirty. Accidents in mines, at worksites, on the river, in homes, and in the streets were a normal part of everyday life. It was every man for himself on the streets of Greater Pittston in 1915, where horses, carriages, automobiles, and trollies ran unfettered by traffic signals or stop signs.

In August of 1915, Mr. Paul Grablick acquired the candy store between Butler and Carroll streets operated by Martin Keating. He used this building at 12 Church Street for his milk dairy. At the outset, he had one horse drawn milk wagon. Every day he had his supply of milk shipped down from Ransom on an early morning Lehigh Valley Railroad train. Religiously he made his rounds to his customers. Raw milk was provided from cans supplied with spigots. As his business gradually expanded, within a few years, he was in a position to build a small pasteurizing plant at the rear of the original dairy.

The Montedoro Society of Pittston was formed in 1916 as a fraternal and civic organization by immigrants who had come to this country from Montedoro, Sicily, making their home in Pittston and working in the coal mines of Wyoming Valley. Among the customs and traditions these immigrants brought with them was the religious tradition of honoring each year, by appropriate festivities, the patron saint of their native village. In 1922 the immigrants from Montedoro decided to commission the construction of a statue of the Mother of the Rosary.

The high point of the celebration is a procession of the Blessed Mother statue through the neighborhoods of Columbus Avenue, Oak, Pine, and Railroad streets. Members accompany the statue on its journey and march with music provided by Cino Paci Band. The procession stops regularly along the route to allow the faithful to pin donations on the statue. This tradition still continues to this day.

Early immigrants from the Carpathian Mountains in Eastern Europe settled in Pittston. They came here with a love of God and church foremost in their lives. They are Byzantine Eastern Rite Catholics. They are of Eastern European Ancestry.

Assisted by the Rev. Myron Volkay of Taylor, a meeting was set for the old Bohemian Hall on North Main Street, Pittston in September 1911. The idea of St. Michael the Archangel Byzantine Catholic Church of Pittston became a reality. Father Volkay served as the first pastor, and the Most Reverend Michael Hoban, D.D. Bishop of Scranton, was the first trustee. Standing majestically above the banks of the Susquehanna River, St. Michael's serves as a monument to God and the faith, love, and sacrifice of the parish's founders and its parishioners.

After Rocco took Maria to the hospital in labor with their eleventh child, Mrs. Esther Tinsley came in the room to help with the delivery. Soon their beautiful and healthy son Ross was born. While Maria was in the hospital, word came that the United States of America declared war with Germany. No one knew how this would affect their lives. Sending men to war always brought home the sad news of casualties. War always changes lives, and everyone in Pittston braced for what could be a long, deadly war.

Soon there was a call to arms and men from Pittston and throughout the nation filled this need by joining the Armed forces. What occurred during this time of battle, World War I, shocked the nation and the world.

# Chapter 13

## WORLD WAR I

World War 1, also known as the Great War was a global war originating in Europe. It led to the mobilization of more than seventy million military personnel, including sixty million Europeans. It was one of the deadliest conflicts in history with an estimated nine million combatant deaths and thirteen million civilian deaths as a direct result of the war. It lasted from July 28th, 1914 to November 11th, 1918.

In 1914, when World War 1 started in Europe, President Woodrow Wilson did not want to enter the war along with the American people's public opinion at the time.

The United States entered the war because of the German's decision to resume the policy of unrestricted submarine warfare and the so called "Zimmerman Telegram." This telegram intercepted by the British, floated the idea of an alliance between Mexico and Germany.

On the evening of April 2nd, 1917, President Woodrow Wilson appeared before a joint session of Congress and asked for a declaration of war against Germany in order to "Make the world safe for Democracy." On April 6th, 1917, the United States declared war on Germany.

The American Red Cross made a major contribution to aid the wounded during World War 1. Within weeks of the threat of war, it dispatched the "Mercy Ship," which brought surgeons, nurses, and medical supplies to Europe. There was no more patriotic organization. When the United States entered the war, the organization began a period of remarkable growth, and by the end of the war, it had become a major humanitarian organization with a record of broad and distinguished service. It equipped several railroad cars as specialized laboratories in case of disease outbreaks. It reserved them for use only by the military, "so that one may be delivered anywhere in the country within twenty-four hours."

William Welch, then President of the National Academy of Sciences, and his colleagues watched as their European counterparts tried to perfect killing devices. This was the first truly scientific war that matched engineers and their abilities to build not just artillery but submarines and physiologists devising or trying to counteract the most lethal poison gas.

President Wilson had been a graduate student at the Johns Hopkins when William Welch had first arrived there and immediately invited him and a few others to the White House. There they proposed to establish a National Research Council to direct all war-related scientific work.

He wanted confidentiality because any preparation for war set off debate. President Wilson created the Council of National Defense, which would lay plans for the virtual government takeover of the production and distribution of economic resources. The membership in the council was comprised of six cabinet secretaries, including the Secretaries of War and the Navy and seven men out of government.

Their plan was to focus on epidemic disease. According to history, more soldiers had often died of disease than in battle or their wounds. They needed as many physicians as possible to serve in the army and navy.

In May of 1918, roughly 16,000 nurses served in the military. According to a report of the Alumnae Association of Nurses at the Pittston Hospital, Pittston, Pennsylvania, nurses responded to the emergency call to serve with the Red Cross in France. Miss Esther Tinsley prepared the nurses assigned to the Army, with what they may encounter to support the troops medically. When possible Miss Katherine Williams, supervisor of the nurses leaving for France, would give a periodic report to Miss Tinsley. This was the nurses first opportunity to serve their country in this capacity, and they left Pittston with honor and pride. All of the doctors and nurses at Pittston Hospital gave them a farewell dinner with prayers and best wishes for a safe tour of duty. After Mass on the day of their departure, they walked from the Saint John the Evangelist Church to the Lehigh Valley Train Station. Walking with them were their families and Miss Esther Tinsley. After they arrived at the station, their families hugged them goodbye. As each nurse boarded the train, Miss Tinsley, with tears in her eyes, gave each nurse a hug. These well-trained Pittston Hospital nurses were among the best in the country and would serve their nation in all circumstances.

In the meantime, the military's need for doctors and nurses only grew. The U. S. Surgeon General was planning for 300,000 hospital beds. The military placed more and more nurses and physicians into cantonments aboard ships into France until it had extracted nearly all the best young physicians and nurses in the country.

On May 18th, 1917, six weeks after the United States declared war on Germany, Congress passed the Selective Service Act, authorizing the federal government to raise a national army for the American entry into World War I through a draft of men between the ages of nineteen and thirty.

On June 5th, 1917, an impromptu celebration broke out in the streets of Pittston. Young men treated the day like a holiday, skipping work and parading en masse to the city's polling stations before partying the day away. Enough booze was sold behind closed doors in Pittston to float a battleship, despite the mayor's hint that it would be extremely unwise for saloon men to open on this day.

The World War I draft was followed by a burst of patriotic pride and eager compliance. Men lined up well before 7 A.M. at all the polling places. By the end of the day, 1,612 had registered in Pittston, double expectations, and more than half the number of registered voters in the city. Authorities had little patience for non-enrollment. On June 6th, the Pittston patrolmen were ordered to arrest any young man unable to produce his registration card.

The earliest draftees to be called to service were seven men from Sebastopol section of Pittston on September 18th, James Horan, George Morris, Edward Hinchcliff, John and Thomas King, Daniel Mullery, and Eugene Philbin. The men were honored at a dinner at the Hotel Reddington, Wilkes-Barre. Philbin had to leave the dinner early to report to New York City to ship out with the submarine L-4.

West Pittston played a special role to America's entry into World War I, and not just because of 500 men who registered. The Garden Village was home to Camp Ricketts, a training center for raw recruits. The camp was built on the tree-lined West Pittston Fairgrounds.

In July of 1917, the fairground was transformed into a full-blown training camp for 1,400 Third Field Artillery recruits. Tents were erected and streets were improved and cleaned every day. Lumber arrived on July 17th for the building of eight mess halls.

After eight weeks, the recruits were ready to move on for further training in Georgia. One hundred women from West Pittston fed a last meal to all 1,400 recruits. They prepared the food in their own kitchens, then organized everything at the West Pittston Presbyterian Church, from where the potato salad, sandwiches, relish, cake, and a slice of ice cream were delivered to the camp in wagons.

The next morning, with the regimental band leading the way, the men marched up Wyoming and Luzerne avenues as an estimated 20,000 people from all over the Wyoming Valley lined the route.

Stores and coal mines were closed, so everyone could attend the farewell parade to the troops. All of the troops were lined up, with Michael Tuminello leading the way playing the bugle. Rocco and Maria, watching the parade with all of their children, were proud to be in the United States of America, and the children saluted the men as they walked by.

At the departure point, men were given time to say good-bye to families and sweethearts. The men entrained into 100 coaches divided into three trains. They traveled to Bethlehem, where they were transferred to the Philadelphia and Reading tracks for the trip south. All that is left of the fairgrounds today is the former Armory in West Pittston.

In 1917 large industries, such as railroads, collieries, and knitting mills, ran their own power plants. Pittston, as did other towns, had its power company, The Citizens Electric Illumination Company.

As coal was vital to the war effort, on December 20th, 1917, William Potter, Federal Fuel administrator for Pennsylvania ordered A.C. Campbell, chairman of the county coal committee, to declare Thursdays and Sundays "lightless nights."

American soldiers under General John Pershing, commander-in-chief of the American Expeditionary Force, didn't arrive in Europe in large numbers until the summer of 1918. On the other hand, by Christmas of 1917, hundreds of young men and boys from Greater Pittston were already in France fighting or at training camps stateside, especially Camp Meade in Maryland. Half of the Pittston contingent training at Camp Meade were furloughed on Friday, December 21st, 1917.

Among those who weren't granted leave were two flyboys with the first U.S. military aviation units, Joseph Devlin of Tompkins Street, who had passed his Army Aviation Corps examination, was on his way to Kelley Field, Texas. Also, Frank Ertle was with the U.S. Navy Aero Corps in Pensacola, Florida. Army nurse Janet Thompson, Broad Street, daughter of Mr. and Mrs. Mungo Thompson, was called to France from Camp Meade so quickly, she couldn't get home to say goodbye.

New young recruits drafted for World War I were being shipped throughout the United States for training before arriving in France. Camp Funston Kansas was one large installation where thousands of new recruits were stationed for training.

After returning home from WWI, Pittston resident, Biagio Manganaro, received the picture, illustrated in Figure 15, from the U.S. government for his service during WWI. After returning home from the war, Biagio went to work in the coal mines in Pittston.

Figure. 15 Honorary picture received by Biagio Manganaro.
(Courtesy of Maria Capolarella-Montante, daughter of Biagio)

# *Chapter 14*
## THE 1918 INFLUENZA

Camp Funston was located in Haskell County, Kansas. In January and February of 1918, Dr. Loring Miner, a country doctor from Haskell County, where Camp Funston was located, encountered a patient with what seemed common symptoms but with unusual severity (violent headache, body aches, high fever, nonproductive cough). These severe symptoms were also evident in other patients and in the cities and towns in the county. This influenza was violent, rapid in its progress through the body and sometimes deadly.

On March 4th, a private at Camp Funston reported ill with influenza. Within three weeks, more than 1,100 soldiers were sick enough to be admitted to a hospital and thousands more needed treatment at infirmaries.

Nearly 791,000 American troops disembarked at Brest, France. Troops from all over the world disembarked there. The first outbreak with high mortality occurred in July, in a replacement detachment of American troops from Camp Pike, Arkansas. They occupied an isolated camp, and the outbreak initially seemed contained. By August 10th, so many French sailors stationed at Brest were hospitalized with influenza and pneumonia that they overwhelmed the naval hospital there, forcing it to close. The death rate among the infected troops began soaring.

At Pittston Hospital, Miss Esther Tinsley received a letter from nurse Katherine Williams. The letter, written hastily, informed Miss Tinsley about the deadly flu in Brest, France. She immediately went into Dr. Underwood's office to inform him of this development. When Miss Tinsley prepared the nurses to treat combat wounds, she never thought they would be battling a deadly flu. Although concerned if the nurses would return safely, Dr. Underwood was also very concerned about the troops returning to America and being carriers of this flu. There was no warning in the recent medical journals or the newspapers. With the soaring population in Pittston and surrounding areas, he was worried about whether they could handle a large influx of patients.

The bottom floor of the Pittston hospital had a large emergency room. Outside the emergency room were other rooms for storage, autopsies, and the morgue. Dr. Underwood wanted everything removed from this area to make an isolation ward ready and available to treat flu cases. He asked Miss Tinsley to order a large quantity of masks, gloves, disinfectant, and body bags. With this request, Miss Tinsley had tears in her eyes but proceeded to do as instructed.

Dr. Underwood immediately called the administrators of Wilkes-Barre City Hospital in Wilkes-Barre, Pennsylvania and Nesbitt Hospital in Kingston, Pennsylvania to inform them of the letter from nurse Katherine Williams. They were very concerned with this news and also prepared for the return of the troops. Although their efforts were warranted, what was to come was a devastating pandemic for the citizens of Luzerne County and a challenge for the medical profession.

It was an unusually warm summer, all the children in Pittston were outside playing in the street or going to the available parks. Rocco and Maria enjoyed this time of year because the warm weather reminded them of Italy. They would make a picnic lunch, sit at the edge of the river, and watch their children swim. At the end of River Street, there was a park for the local children to play ball. On Sunday the whole day would be spent with family.

On a warm Saturday night with the door open, Rocco and Maria could hear the Keating Brothers or the Columbian Band playing at the armory. Usually the armory would have its back door open to let some cool night air in for the couples' dancing. Rocco pulled Maria close to him and held her for a while. They began to dance. The smell of her hair and the curves of her body excited Rocco. Maria was the woman he loved and desired, the woman that made his life complete, the woman that bore his children. All of their dreams came true. It seemed each year so many good things happened to them. Coming to America, living in Oregon Section, Pittston, and the birth of their children made everything worthwhile. When needed family and friends in the surrounding area were always ready to help. Through their hard work, they earned sufficient money to provide for the children. They accomplished their dreams and desires to make America their home.

In the meantime, the flu was spreading in the United States.

At Commonwealth Pier in Boston, the Navy operated a "receiving ship" that was actually a barracks where as many as 7,000 sailors in transit ate and slept in what the Navy called "grossly overcrowded" quarters. On August 27th, two sailors reported to sick bay with influenza, on August 28th, eight more sailors reported ill, and on August 29th, fifty-eight men were admitted. As in Brest, France, men began to die.

On September 7th, a soldier from D company, 42nd infantry was sent to the hospital. He ached to the extent that he screamed when he was touched and he was delirious. He was diagnosed as having meningitis.

A day went by, two days, then suddenly noted an Army report, "Stated briefly, the influenza…occurred as an explosion."

On September 7th, 300 sailors arrived from Boston at the Philadelphia Navy Yard. Four days after the arrival of the sailors from Boston to Philadelphia Navy Yard, nineteen sailors reported ill with symptoms of influenza. By September 15th, the virus made 600 sailors and marines sick enough to require hospitalization. The Navy began sending ill sailors to the Pennsylvania Hospital at Eighth and Spruce streets. On September 17th, five doctors and fourteen nurses in that civilian hospital suddenly collapsed. None had exhibited any prior symptoms. One moment they felt normal; the next, they were being carried in agony to hospital beds. As Philadelphia was erupting, so was the Great Lakes Naval Training Station.

In Philadelphia the most terrifying aspect of the epidemic was the piling up of the bodies and the city's ability to handle them. It was forced to bury people without coffins, in mass graves, and soon began using steam shovels to dig the graves.

Pennsylvania was one of the hardest hit states with what was known at that time as the Spanish Flu. The origin of this disease is unknown.

The scourge invaded Pennsylvania about the middle of September 1918, attacking simultaneously widely-separated communities. On October 1st, 1918 in Luzerne County, the Department of Health issued orders directing the closing of all moving-picture houses, theaters, and places of amusement in general, the public assemblages be discontinued, that funerals be privately conducted, and that all bar-rooms and wholesale liquor establishments be closed. The matter of closing schools, churches, and Sunday schools was left to the discretion of local authorities.

Owing to the absence of many local physicians and trained nurses in the military and naval services of the United States, the Red Cross of Wyoming Valley issued an appeal on October 3rd, 1918 for trained nurses and for women with some nursing experience, to register with the chapter for service in combating the disease.

Dr. Charles H. Miner of Wilkes-Barre, Pennsylvania, who at the time had been the County Medical Inspector of the State Department of Health for Luzerne County, was to take full charge of the organization and co-ordinate all work in District No. 5, composed of Luzerne and Columbia counties, with headquarters in Wilkes-Barre. A General Committee, consisting of forty-two people, was formed "for the purpose of taking steps for combating influenza" and met in the Wilkes-Barre Chamber of Commerce on the evening of October 9th, 1918. Some of the attendees were Miss Esther Tinsley, Dr. J. A. Hilbert, Dr. S. Underwood, and William J. Peck, of Pittston, and R. A. Mulhall, of West Pittston. Each gave a report of their town. Dr. Underwood and Miss Tinsley spoke of conditions in Exeter, Luzerne County, where nearly 300 cases then existed. After the reports, the committee decided more help would be needed.

Pittston Hospital, Wilkes-Barre Hospital, and Nesbitt Hospital could not handle the influx of flu patients, and the doctors decided to establish an Emergency Hospital in Wilkes-Barre. The armory of the 9th Regiment, National Guard of Pennsylvania, located on South Main Street, was selected for that purpose. Within the next six weeks, seven more emergency hospitals were located in Wanamie, Catawissa, Exeter, Hazleton, Dupont, Nanticoke, and Plains.

Anthony C. Campbell, Esq., County Fuel Administrator, told of the serious conditions with respect to the mining industry in the 5th District, and declared that the output of anthracite coal was being seriously affected by the pandemic. Reports from large coal mining companies showed that 28,000 to 30,000 tons of coal had been lost to the industry on account of the influenza. Six thousand mine workers were ill with the disease, thus reducing the daily output of anthracite coal by 15,000 tons, or at the rate of 300,000 tons per month.

Dr. Mengel, Chief Surgeon of the Lehigh Valley Coal Company, placed the nurses of that organization at the disposal of the community and suggested that school teachers be employed to help in the work of caring for the sick.

Inside the mines, men collapsed, and within a few hours, were dead. Many had to be put in the coal cars to be taken from the mine. Pittston, Pennsylvania, like other outlying towns, looked deserted.

People were afraid to leave their homes or apartments. All of the schools and churches were closed. The undertakers were busy picking up bodies left at the end of each street.

On October 28th, 1918, Rocco walked home from the mines and collapsed in the door of the apartment. Maria and the children put him on the bed near the stove. He could barely talk or breathe. Not knowing if he could see or hear, Maria held his hand and told him how much she loved him. The crying children said goodbye to their father. Dr. Underwood was coming out of a nearby home, and Michael asked him to come to their house to see his father. Dr. Underwood knew by the first sight of Rocco that he would not live much longer.

He explained, "There is nothing anyone could do to help the influenza victims. There isn't a serum or vaccine." The next day, on October 29th, 1918, Rocco passed away in the arms of his dear beloved Maria.

Graziano Funeral Home was located on South Main Street in Pittston. Maria saw Mr. Cesar Graziano at the neighbor's house collecting a body. She asked Mr. Graziano if he would take Rocco's body to the funeral home. He said yes and soon came with paperwork for Maria to sign. He explained they were not allowed to have a wake because of the flu epidemic. Five days later, Graziano's funeral cars came to pick up Maria and others attending the funeral. Everyone had to stay in the cars as the Graziano brothers took the casket to the assigned grave. The family was allowed a few minutes to say a prayer.

*Chapter 15*

## SAINT MICHAEL'S SCHOOL FOR BOYS

After the death of their father Rocco, cousin Michael helped Michael and Dominick apply for work in the coal mine. Soon they started as their father before them, to work as laborers at the Pennsylvania Coal Company. Life was much worse for Maria and the children to survive without a husband and father. Although their large family was there to help as much as possible, it was still a struggle to survive. Many families suffered multiple deaths from the flu and some were not able to exist on their own. A small amount of money from a relief fund was given monthly for six months to each family who had a wage earner die from the flu. This money could be used for food or rent. In 1919 the flu again killed many more people in the United States and Pittston. The death total from the flu in Luzerne County was 34,043. The total number of children made orphans in Luzerne County was 2,390.

After the six months, Maria realized it would be too hard for her to continue living in the apartment. She met with Father Gislon at Our Lady of Mount Carmel Church to discuss what was available to her from the Catholic Church. Father Gislon suggested that some of the children could go to Saint Michael's School for Boys, located at Hoban Heights in Wyoming County, Pennsylvania. At first Maria didn't feel she could separate herself from the children. Maria would be able to live with her parents, however, there wasn't enough room for all the children. She discussed it with her family and gave serious thought about the decision to send Anthony and Rocco to Saint Michael's School for Boys. Their cousin Joseph Policare went to Saint Michael's because of the death of his father.

Oregon Section had a large community of Italian families, and many wanted to have their own Italian Church in this area. The Catholic Church secured land at the corner of west Oak and

Tompkins Street to build Saint Rocco's Church. Joseph Santangelo, a stone mason, laid the block for the foundation of the church. He was helped by Salvatore Scalzo, Joseph Mastruzzo, Michael Policare, Joseph Sperazza, and others who worked in the mines and then came home and helped prepare the foundation for the church.

Within a few months, Saint Rocco's Church was dedicated with Reverend John DePietro as the first pastor. Yearly processions are conducted for Saint Rocco, the Mother of Sorrows, and the Mother of the Rosary. The processors carry the statues through the neighborhood as the faithful line the streets. The statues are lowered, and people attach monetary donations to a sash on the statue. The parades are accompanied by the Cino's Paci band. Year after year, the cries of "Viva, San Rocco" as the members of the Mutual Aid Society of Saint Rocco's hoist the statue of Saint Rocco on their shoulders and processed over the hilly streets of the Oregon section.

After giving much thought about sending the boys to Saint Michael's School for Boys, Maria and her cousin Rosaria met with Father Gislon at Our Lady of Mount Carmel Church and made the arrangements for Anthony, Rocco, and cousin Joseph to leave Pittston to attend this school. She wanted to wait until after they attended the homecoming parade for the returning soldiers of World War I.

The people of Pittston were on edge awaiting the arrival of the heroic boys of Battery B,109th Field Artillery, who had been representing them on fields of France and Belgium in the Great War for humanity. First Lieutenant, Leo Tierney of Pittston, commander of Battery B, 109th Field Artillery, sent the PITTSTON GAZETTE a partial official roster of the Battery.

At 10:30 A.M., the blaring of gongs and the ringing of bells announced to the people of the valley the arrival of the 109th regiment at Glen Summit. They continued to sound while the special train bearing the returning heroes moved slowly down the mountain to Wilkes-Barre.

The local boys put their feet on Pittston soil at 11:15 A.M., on May 20th, 1919 when they stepped from the special Lehigh Valley train at the Pittston Junction. Tremendous crowds of people from Pittston and the surrounding towns lined the tracks of the Lehigh Valley Railroad to catch their first glimpse of the soldiers. Even greater crowds were on Main Street awaiting their arrival.

The proposed route was to march down north Main Street to the Water Street bridge, cross to Susquehanna Avenue, up Exeter Avenue to Spring Street, down Luzerne Avenue, again crossing Water Street bridge, continue down south Main Street to the Armory.

It was a glorious day, the likes of which had never before been witnessed in the community. Battery B,109th Field Artillery, achieved a notable record for loyalty and valor in the Great War, and the celebration marked their home-coming was in every respect in keeping with their magnificent conduct on the field of battle.

The proprietors decorated the business places along Main Street and the adjacent side streets. American flags, flags of the allied nations, bunting, and varied colors of electric lights, and large banners constituted the main decoration scheme. Haltzel's Furniture was the most elegantly decorated place of business.

Other businesses finely decorated with large banners were The Roman and Dreamland theaters, Pittston Dry Goods Store, Gompertz, The Peoples Bank, Dime Bank, Miners' Hall, First National Bank, Evans Brothers, Drury's, and Louis Schiffman's Shoe Store.

Maria and the children stood in front of Anthony Forlenza's Confection Store holding their balloons and waving their small flags. The first person seated in the front of an open Jeep was Pittston's hero Leo Tierney, who was accompanied by other highly decorated uniformed men. State Troopers walked along the jeep, and Mr. Tierney waved and saluted to everyone.

The children were all excited when they saw their neighbor, Giuseppe Tuminelli, proudly playing the bugle. Marching behind him was the 109th Regiment. Numerous bands from Pittston and the surrounding towns proceeded down Main Street. The Red Cross Motor Corps ended the parade. Everyone cheered to let them know how thankful they were for their service to their country. Gratefully all of the Pittston Hospital's nurses returned safely. Although some men from Pittston were wounded or lost their lives for their country, it was a fine celebration.

Kresge's gave all children a free ice cream. After eating the ice cream, Maria and the children walked back to their apartment. It was time for Maria to let her two sons, Anthony and Rocco, know they would be going to Saint Michael's School for Boys. She explained it was a new school located a few miles away, just for boys whose fathers were missing or deceased. She assured them they would be fine and well-taken care of by the priests and nuns. They cried because they did not want to leave the family. Maria continued hugging them and telling them they would be fine; they finally accepted her decision.

The following week, Father Gislon came to the apartment to take the boys to Saint Michael's School for Boys. They hugged everyone goodbye and boarded the train with Father Gislon. The train traveled along the river for fourteen miles, and on the right-hand side, they could see a large, three-story red brick building with a bell tower on top. They were excited, anxious, and apprehensive to enter the school far away from Pittston and their mother. They trusted Father Gislon, and he assured them everything would be all right and he would come to visit them on a regular basis. He would give a report to their mother on their progress and any problems would be discussed with her.

*FIGURE 16. SIGN AT THE ENTRANCE TO SAINT MICHAEL'S SCHOOL FOR BOYS*

The Most Reverend Michael J. Hoban, D.D. second Bishop of Scranton, founded St. Michael's School for Boys on a tract of land, which witnessed some of the most grueling pioneer battles in the northeastern part of our country. Situated on a picturesque knoll overlooking the Susquehanna River along historic Sullivan Trail, St. Michael's was opened on October 26th, 1916 for seventy-five boys from the Diocese of Scranton. Later this area was called Hoban Heights.

Believing that it was not enough to provide food and clothing for underprivileged boys and relying on the generosity of his people, Bishop Hoban erected an institution that would mold the characters of boys who were more deprived than depraved, develop the minds of the homeless, unhappy boys and train the hands of future craftsman. The early days of St. Michael's were difficult. The water supply was inadequate, the roads inaccessible for the large part of the year, the farm lands neglected and the institutional program undeveloped. Although much had been accomplished in the way of construction providing the building with the best in heating and refrigeration, there remained a gigantic task for the first director, Reverend Eugene P. Caulfield. Together with the Sisters, Servants of the Immaculate Heart of Mary, Father Caulfield laid the foundation for a permanent child care facility.

*FIGURE 17. FATHER EUGENE P. CAULFIELD, FIRST ADMINISTRATOR OF THE SCHOOL*

Upon entering Saint Michael's, Anthony, Rocco, and cousin Joseph were greeted by Father Eugene P. Caulfield and Sister Mary Inviolata, the first principal of the school. They were very welcoming and shook hands with the three boys.

On the wall entrance was a large wooden crucifix with candle sconces on each side. To the left, there was a picture of the Blessed Mother and Saint Joseph. Father Gislon began to tell them of the hardships of many families in Pittston and he was sure there would be more boys entering Saint Michael's. Sister Mary brought the boys into the cafeteria area for some lunch.

The boys were quiet and felt very out of place in such a large building. Also, they were already missing their mother, brothers, sisters, and Pittston.

When Sister Mary Inviolata came back to the foyer, Father Gislon requested that the boys stay together. Sister Mary could understand this request and assured Father Gislon they would be placed together. She had to rearrange the sleeping area, so the two brothers and their cousin would have beds side by side. The room to the right of the foyer was a large area with all the beds in rows. In front of the beds, there was a chair to sit and a small box for anything the boys wanted to store. Beneath each bed was a drawer for their new clothes and toiletries, which would be supplied by the school.

FIGURE 18. DORMITORY AREA

All of the boys came into the dining room located on the left side of the foyer for dinner at six o'clock. After dinner Father Caulfield talked to the boys and also introduced any new child. That night Father Caufield introduced the two Policare brothers and their cousin. Everyone welcomed them, and Father Caulfield assigned two boys to show them around the building and grounds, the classrooms, lavatory, showers, and nurse's office. The classrooms were located on the second floor, and the nun's quarters were on the third floor.

The following day, the boys were put into classrooms, depending on their age. This was the only time they would be separated. The three boys soon acclimated to their new school and made friends easily. As the months passed and the warm summer weather arrived, the boys were separated into teams to play baseball. Some of the boys weren't familiar with playing ball, but Father Caulfield insisted everyone learn the game. Mr. Joseph Kosco, a caretaker and handyman who lived nearby, was usually the referee.

When Mr. Kosco was unavailable because he was working on the land or maintaining the building, Father Caulfield refereed. He made sure everyone was in the game and had a chance at bat. He named the teams, and whatever team won, he would give a special prize. He also made the boys laugh. He thought a smiling child was a happy child. Whenever Father Caulfield was around, everyone had a good time, and they felt as though he was a father to them. He was always there to counsel the boys on many different subjects. His office door was always open to talk to a child. For twenty years, he labored to build the institution's program and expand its facilities, but his most important duty was the welfare of the children.

For the first few weeks, Maria didn't hear anything from the boys. The second month, she received a letter written by Anthony telling her about their experiences at the school. They were doing fine, and she realized she made the right decision for them.

Winter time at Saint Michael's was always a lot of fun sleigh riding down the large hills in front of the building. When Father Caulfield was available, he joined the fun. One day he was going outside and he noticed the three boys on crutches with braces on their legs, looking out the windows watching the other boys sleigh ride down the hills. Father Caulfield asked them why they weren't outside sleigh riding.

They replied, "We can't sleigh ride because of our crutches." Father Caulfield put on their coats, hats, and boots. He helped the boys to the top of the hill. He had a few boys bring the sleighs up the hill. He put one large boy in front, then he put the boy without his crutches behind the boy in front, finally Father Caulfield hopped on the sleigh in back to hold on to the boy. They went down the hill together. It was a fun time for everyone, and Father Caulfield let these boys know they could do anything.

Christmas was one week away, and the boys were decorating the tree. The Policare's were homesick with the thought of not being with their mother at Christmas. On the night before Christmas Eve, after everyone was sleeping, Anthony and Rocco decided to leave Saint Michael's and walk home for Christmas. They dressed warm and left after everyone fell asleep. They followed the railroad, and a few hours later, they were very tired. It seemed closer when they were in the train, but they kept going. All of a sudden, a fox was before them growling and showing his teeth. They were scared and held on to each other. They cried because they knew they couldn't run away. At that point, they heard a gunshot and saw the farmer with his gun. He saved them. The farmer asked if they wanted some breakfast, and they said yes. They were in the warm house eating breakfast when they heard the farmer calling the police to let them know they were at his house. They ran out of the house quickly and followed the railroad to Pittston. Upon arriving in the Oregon Section of Pittston, they saw their mother, Father Gislon, and the policeman. Tearfully they hugged their mother. Maria asked Father Gislon if they could stay for Christmas. Father Gislon agreed. It was a Christmas they would always remember.

One day Father Caulfield was looking out the second-floor window and he could see a woman in the distance walking with a child towards St. Michael's. He called Sister Mary to unlock the door to welcome her. She knocked on the door, and Father Caulfield and Sister Mary welcomed her into the foyer at St. Michael's. She explained to them that she could no longer provide for her son, Sam, and wanted him to enter St. Michael's. After a long conversation with her, Father Caulfield said her son is welcome and he would be provided for until she could come back for him or when he reached the age to be allowed to leave St. Michael's. It was a tearful goodbye with her son, but she knew she could no longer take care of him.

The next few months were very hard for Sam. At night Sister Mary would walk through the large room where the boys were sleeping. She had a room off to the side with a bed if a child needed her. Sam was one of these children.

At night she was dressed in a long white dress with a short white veil. One night, when Sam was crying, Sister Mary asked if he wanted to go to the kitchen with her for some ice cream.

He followed her to the kitchen, and they talked for a long time while eating ice cream. She assured him that everything would be fine and someday he would be old enough to leave St. Michael's and reunite again with his mother. She decided to move his bed next to the two Policare brothers because they seemed to always be laughing and having fun. In fact the next day, she mentioned to them she thought they needed another brother. Soon Sam was in with group and was able to blend in with all the boys. In time all the boys would leave St. Michael's and either return to their families or go out into the world alone with what they learned at St. Michael's. Many came back to visit St. Michael's with their families. St. Michael's is a story of love, courage, and sacrifice. It is a story of dedicated priests and sisters, a story of joys and sorrows, a story of victories and defeats.

After the smaller children were asleep, Maria sat by the stove with tears in her eyes. She thought about her early life in Calabria, Italy and falling in love with Rocco. When they went for a walk, he knelt down on one knee and he asked her to marry him. They were so happy and in love. After the birth of two children in Italy, they boarded the ship to America. After two weeks on the ship, in the steerage compartment, they arrived at Ellis Island. She remembered how worried they were if they would pass the exams and be granted entry to the greatest country in the world. At Ellis Island, most immigrants were accepted to enter and make America their homeland. When boarding the train in New Jersey and arriving in Pittston, Pennsylvania, she could still hear the new immigrant sitting alongside them playing his harmonica. Pittston was a melting pot of immigrants with all different languages being spoken. Everyone had their own customs and attended their own church. Even though there were differences, they always made an effort to welcome new immigrants. She remembered the Jews graciously extending credit to immigrants from all different countries. Most of all, she thought about the kindness of the neighbors in Oregon Section, who shared their food with new arriving immigrants that needed help.

She cried as she remembered the laughter and joy they experienced with the birth of their eleven children, the excitement when Rocco would bring her flowers he picked from an open field, the nights they danced to the music they could hear from the Armory. As Maria cried, all these memories came to her mind. Life would never be the same, but she had faith in God and prayed for her children. She instilled in her children to always remember their wonderful and caring father.

The boys applied what they learned at St. Michaels and led productive lives in all different professions. Carlo and Joseph settled with their families in New Jersey. Rocco and Anthony lived the rest of their lives in Pittston. Rosa died giving birth, but her child Mary survived. Victoria also died giving birth. Michael and Dominick worked all of their lives in the coal mines. Ross moved to the state of Oregon with his family. Frank lived in Las Vegas, Nevada. Maria lived thirty years after Rocco's death. In her last years, she was cared for by and lived with her only remaining daughter, Laura Schillaci and family. Maria never remarried as Rocco was her soul mate, her one true love. In 1948, her Life in the New World, Pittston, Pennsylvania was over, and a new eternal chapter with Rocco began.

<h1 style="text-align:center">Bibliography</h1>

## Books


Anbinder, Tyler. *City of Dreams; The 400-Year Epic History of Immigrant New York.* New York: Houghton Mifflin Harcourt, 2016.

Azzarelli, Margo L., and Marnie Azzarelli. *Labor Unrest In Scranton.* Charleston, South Carolina: The History Press, 2016.

Barry, John M. *The Great Influenza.* New York: Penguin Group, 2005.

Brauer, Norm. *Narrative of Northern Electric Street Railway Company, Scranton and Binghamton Railway Company, Narrative of the Dalton Street Railway Company.* Factoryville, Pennsylvania: *Print-Ed Products,* May 2005.

Bussacco, James and Charles MCCarthy. *History of the City of Pittston, History of Pittston's Coal Mining Era Mining Accidents, McCarthy's History of Wyoming Valley,* Wyoming Observer<Unpublished> 1995.

Daughters of the American Revolution, Black Diamond Cookbook

Gallagher, John P. *A Century of History,1868-1968. Diocese of Scranton.* Scranton, Pennsylvania: The Haddon Craftsman, *1968.*

Glahn, Bryan. *Mining Disasters of the Wyoming Valley.* Charleston, South Carolina: Aarcadia Publishing, 2016.

Levin, Marjorie, Sheldon Spear, and Gladys Weinberger. *The Jews of Wilkes-Barre; 150 years (1845-1995) in the Wyoming Valley of Pennsylvania.* Wilkes-Barre, Pennsylvania: Jewish Community Center of Wyoming Valley, 1999.

Longo, Stephanie. *Italians of Northeastern Pennsylvania*. Charleston, South Carolina: Arcadia Publishing, 2004.

Polk, R.L. and Company. Pittston City Directories: 1892, 1896, 1897

Richards, John Stuart. *Early Coal Mining in the Anthracite Region*. Charleston, South Carolina: Arcadia Publishing, 2002.

Rohrbecks, Benson W., *Scranton Trolleys*. West Chester, Pennsylvania: Ben Rohrbeck Traction Publications, 1999.

Wolensky, Robert P. and William A. Hastie, Sr. *Anthracite Labor Wars*. Easton, Pennsylvania: Canal History and Technology, 2013.

## JOURNALS/BOOKLETS/MAGAZINES

Greater Pittston Journal Volume 3, Issue 1 Winter 2016, Eric B. McKitish, New Synagogue of the Jewish People Nears Completion (reproduced from the Pittston Gazette, 6 January 1916)

Greater Pittston Journal, Volume 2, Issue 4 Autumn 2015, Eric B. McKitish, The Changing Pittston by Charles A. McCarthy, (reproduced from the Pittston Gazette, 28 October 1965)

Happening Magazine – Lauren Beppler – Saint John Evangelical Lutheran Church -February 2016, pp.94,96

Annual Report of Alumnae Association Meeting Journal, Pittston Hospital, June 6, 1917, Greater Pittston Historical Society

Saint Michael's 50th Anniversary Booklet

## NEWSPAPERS

August 4, 1910. "Presidential Visit, Dynamite Salute". Pittston Gazette, Special to the New York Times

Anonymous. August 25, 1910. "Dime Bank Getting Ready to be Built". Pittston Gazette, p1

Anonymous. May 20, 1919 and May 21, 1919. "A Hundred Thousand Welcomes to Pittston's own Battery B". Pittston Gazette, p1

McCarthy, Jr., Charles A. August 2, 1950." Broad Street Theater and Opera House". Pittston Gazette.p5 Section C

McCarthy, Jr., Charles A. August 2, 1950. "Y.M.C.A." Pittston Gazette. Section D

McCarthy, Jr., Charles A. August 2, 1950. "First National Bank". Pittston Gazette. Section D, p6

McCarthy, Jr., Charles A. August 2, 1950. "Joseph Sordoni, Banks in the Flat Iron Building". Pittston Gazette. Section D, p6

McCarthy, Jr., Charles A. October 28, 1965. "The Changing Pittston". Pittston Gazette

Petronak, Andy. August 4, 1985. "Brogan's Half Century". Sunday Dispatch. Page 11

Sibilano, Joseph Reverend. August 1, 2012. "Saint Rocco's Church History". Sunday Dispatch

Smiles, Jack. September 22, 2014. "Austin S. Powers" citizensvoice.com

Smiles, Jack. January 18, 2015. "Roosevelt Thrilled City Residents with Surprise Visit".

Citizens Voice. pittstonprogress.com

Smiles, Jack. September 15, 2016. "The Lehigh Valley Railroad Station in Pittston was the State of the Art 1964". Citizens Voice. Greater pittstonprogress.com

Ackerman, Ed. September 18, 2016. "Church Founded in Pittston in 1776". Citizens Voice, Greater Pittston Progress

Smiles, Jack. October 9, 2016. "Remembering the Eagles". Citizens Voice Greater Pittston Progress

Smiles, Jack. March 12, 2017. "At the Core of the Community". Citizens Voice Greater Pittston Progress p2

Smiles, Jack. May 14, 2017. "Area Men Rushed to Sign Up During World War 1 Draft". Citizens Voice Greater Pittston Progress

Smiles, Jack. September 3, 2017. "Oddly enough, Thistle Lodge seeks no Recognition for Good Deeds". Citizens Voice Greater Pittston Progress p2

Caprari, Julio and Jack Smiles. September 17, 2017. "Dime Bank". Citizens Voice, Greater Pittston Progress p2

Smiles, Jack. November 12, 2017. "Ministry Milestone". Citizens Voice Greater Pittston Progress p1

Minsavage, Judy. December 3, 2017. "Peeking into the Past, Saint James Church".

Sunday Dispatch

Smiles, Jack. December 24, 2017. 'Looking Back on a Wartime Christmas in 1917". Citizens Voice Greater Pittston Progress p2

R.L. Polk Directories 1892- Luzerne County Historical Society

The Citizens Voice

Greater Pittston Progress

Newspapers.com

The Pittston Gazette

The Times Leader

## Interviews

Ann Conroy – History of Oregon Section July 24, 2017

Denise Dommermuth and Eileen Williams 1998 - Family History

Frances Valenti Tigue-May 8, 2017

Thomas Supey Jr. July 10, 2017

Ellis Island Immigration Center Visit -Powderly Collection-Catholic University of America November 16, 2016

## Websites

www.wikipedia.org Calimera, Italy

www.mtholyoke.edu History of Italian Immigration, Alexandra Molnar 12-10-2010

www.statueofliberty.org History of Ellis Island

www.cnn.com Inside Ellis Island Abandoned Hospitals, Aaron Cooper CNN, 01-27-2016

www.pittstoncity.org

www.britannica.com Great Famine, Joel Mokyr

www.italiamerica.org Southern Italian Immigration, Nicola Colella

www.thebreakerboysbrianeicher.weebly.com

www.umcpittston.org

www.mattivifamily.com/journey_to_america.html Journey to America April 2016 www.wikipedia.org History of Wilkes-Barre Pennsylvania, History of Scranton Pennsylvania

www.duchessoutlet.com Pittston Stove Building

www.italythisway.com History of San Cataldo

www.americanlibrary.org

www.lvrrhs.org Lehigh Valley Railroad

www.luzernecounty.org History of Luzerne County, Welsh immigration

www.nlm.nih.gov The National Library of Medicine, Report from the General Committee, Luzerne County Influenza Epidemic 1918-1919

www.ingramcontent.com/pod-product-compliance
Lightning Source LLC
Chambersburg PA
CBHW071337150726
47997CB00002B/757